The New
Enchantment of America

FLORIDA

By Allan Carpenter

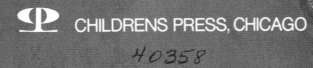 CHILDRENS PRESS, CHICAGO

ACKNOWLEDGMENTS

For assistance in the preparation of the revised edition, the author thanks:
TIM OLSSON and DOT ADAMS, State of Florida Department of Commerce.

American Airlines—Anne Vitaliano, Director of Public Relations; *Capitol Historical Society*, Washington, D. C. ; *Newberry Library,* Chicago, Dr. Lawrence Towner, Director; *Northwestern University Library*, Evanston, Illinois; *United Airlines*—John P. Grember, Manager of Special Promotions; Joseph P. Hopkins, Manager, News Bureau.

UNITED STATES GOVERNMENT AGENCIES: *Department of Agriculture*—Robert Hailstock, Jr., Photography Division, Office of Communication; Donald C. Schuhart, Information Division, Soil Conservation Service. *Army*—Doran Topolosky, Public Affairs Office, Chief of Engineers, Corps of Engineers. *Department of Interior*—Louis Churchville, Director of Communications; EROS Space Program—Phillis Wiepking, Community Affairs; Charles Withington, Geologist; Mrs. Ruth Herbert, Information Specialist; Bureau of Reclamation; National Park Service—Fred Bell and the individual sites; Fish and Wildlife Service—Bob Hines, Public Affairs Office. *Library of Congress*—Dr. Alan Fern, Director of the Department of Research; Sara Wallace, Director of Publications; Dr. Walter W. Ristow, Chief, Geography and Map Division; Herbert Sandborn, Exhibits Officer. *National Archives*—Dr. James B. Rhoads, Archivist of the United States; Albert Meisel, Assistant Archivist for Educational Programs; David Eggenberger, Publications Director; Bill Leary, Still Picture Reference; James Moore, Audio-Visual Archives. *United States Postal Service*—Herb Harris, Stamps Division.

For assistance in the preparation of the first edition, the author thanks:
Dr. Dorothy Dodd, State Librarian; R.J. Seabolt, Florida Development Commission; Christine Genovar, St. Augustine; Stephen Schmidt, Martin County Historical Society; Don Poindexter, Sunken Gardens; William R. Diehl, Silver Springs; Florida Board of Parks and Historic Memorials; Florida Board of Forestry; Florida Citrus Commission; Florida Department of Agriculture; St. Augustine and St. Johns County Chamber of Commerce; Jacksonville University; Orange Blossom Trail Association.

Illustrations on the preceding pages:
Cover photograph: Macaws in Busch Gardens, C. Johnsos
Page 1: Commemorative stamps of historic interest
Pages 2-3: Sea oats on sand dunes at Vilano Beach, St. Augustine Harbor, Department of the Army, Jacksonville District, Corps of Engineers
Page 3 (Map): USDI Geological Survey
Pages 4-5: Miami Area, EROS Space Photo, USDI Geological Survey, EROS Data Center

Project Editor, Revised Edition:
    Joan Downing
Assistant Editor, Revised Edition:
    Mary Reidy

Library of Congress Cataloging in Publication Data

Carpenter, John Allan, 1917-
    Florida

    (His The new enchantment of America)
    SUMMARY: An introduction to the history, geography, natural resources, people, and places of interest of the Sunshine State.
    1. Florida—Juvenile literature.
[1. Florida] I. Title. II. Series.
F311.3.C3 1978   975.9   78-8108
ISBN 0-516-04109-6

Contents

A True Story to Set the Scene

The great bells had just finished their silvery melody. For a moment the enchanting garden was silent. Then the voice of a bird rang out, sounding like the peal of a smaller bell. Those who heard it were astonished. It was the voice of a nightingale, and there were no more nightingales in Florida.

Almost every fairy tale has its nightingale, and this is a kind of modern, true fairy tale.

Like all such stories it began "once upon a time" when a poor immigrant boy came to America. Edward Bok worked hard and used his brilliant mind to become one of the best known and most successful publishers and authors in America. He became editor of the *Ladies' Home Journal* and wrote the Pulitzer Prize book, *The Americanization of Edward Bok.*

He became a wealthy man and decided to use some of his wealth to enhance the beauty of Florida, his favorite state.

Edward Bok created the Mountain Lake Sanctuary, a beautiful garden on Iron Mountain, one of the highest points in Florida. In the middle of the garden, he built a soaring carillon spire. It is called the Singing Tower because it is said to have the finest set of carillon bells in the world. Of the seventy-one bells, the smallest weighs 12 pounds (5.4 kilograms) and the heaviest weighs a mighty 11 tons (10 metric tons). Their notes range over four and a half octaves. The tower, reaching 230 feet (over 70 meters) into the air, is decorated with pink and gray marble and statuary.

Many of those who visit the gardens of the Singing Tower feel as if they had come into an outdoor cathedral.

On one of his visits to Europe, Edward Bok was so pleased with the singing of the nightingales that he felt his Singing Tower would not be complete without the voices of these wonderful birds. So Mr. Bok arranged to have a large number of nightingales brought to his

*Opposite: Closeup of Bok Tower in
Mountain Lake Sanctuary, Lake Wales.*

Florida sanctuary. For some time their voices added a choir to the outdoor cathedral. The climate was too warm and tropical, however, and the nightingales did not do well. Finally, sadly, the last one died.

Strangely, however, people continued to hear their song, as if the spirits of the birds continued to sing. The truth soon became known. The clever mockingbird had listened intently to this foreign vocal coach, and when the last of the favored nightingales had died, the mockingbird took over, adding the beautiful song of the nightingale to its many other calls.

Gardens in Mountain Lake Sanctuary. The "Singing Tower" is in the background.

Lay of the Land

"I can see the whole state of Florida just laid out like a map. It's beautiful. I can see clear back along the gulf coast."

These were the words of a famous explorer. But this was no early Spanish discoverer sailing along a palm-fringed shore. This was an explorer of space, whirling through the darkness of the outer reaches—America's first man in orbit, John Glenn.

If the early explorers could have examined the photographs of Florida taken by John Glenn, they would have been able to avoid incredible hardships.

They would have seen clearly that Florida was not an island, as some of them had thought. The sheltered harbors and inlets of rivers they wanted so much to find would have appeared to them instantly.

It is only one of the lesser marvels of the age of space that the work of a moment could record forever facts that had taken more than four hundred of the preceding years to learn.

Glenn's photos clearly show the unusual nature of Florida's formation and location.

Here is a land that by all the usual calculations probably should not be there at all. Why this low peninsula, five hundred miles (more than eight hundred kilometers) long, should have slowly emerged from the sea is a question on which there is still disagreement. Will it continue to rise, or will it sink, centuries from now, back into the sea?

The Florida of today is one of the most unusual of all our states in its physical makeup. At its highest point it is only 345 feet (about 105 meters) above sea level, and most of the state is only a few feet above the reach of the ocean.

Water is the distinguishing feature of Florida. Salt waters of the sea encircle the state; beneath much of Florida's surface lies a vast lake of fresh water, fed by the runoff of heavy rains. In many parts of the state this water, in the form of springs, bursts forth above the surface in mighty torrents.

Seventeen of the nation's seventy-five first-magnitude springs surge up in Florida. A first-magnitude spring is one with a flow of a hundred cubic feet (nearly three cubic meters) of water every second. Fifty second-magnitude springs are also found in Florida.

Florida even has a spring in the ocean, three miles (nearly five kilometers) east of Crescent Beach, near Jacksonville. It bubbles fresh water up through the salt water in such volume that the sea is often free of salt at that spot. The deepest spring in Florida is Wakulla, south of Tallahassee. It is 185 feet (about 56 meters) deep.

There are more lakes in Florida than in any other state. More than thirty thousand of Florida's lakes have been officially named, and many more have not yet been christened.

Lake Okeechobee is the second largest freshwater lake entirely within the United States. Other prominent lakes include Lake Seminole, Chain o' Lakes, Silver Lake, and Orange Lake with its floating islands.

The mightiest of Florida's 166 rivers is the great St. Johns. It is one of the few rivers in the United States that flows north. Though the St. Johns River has its source only 12 miles (19 kilometers) from the sea, it flows 250 miles (about 400 kilometers) along the coastline before it reaches the ocean.

Two other Florida rivers are among the major streams of the country—the Suwannee and the Apalachicola. Other well-known Florida rivers are the Withlacoochee, Hillsborough, Kissimmee, and Caloosahatchee. The St. Marys River is extremely crooked. In one area it flows for 170 miles (about 274 kilometers) over a straight distance of only 65 miles (about 105 kilometers).

There are no mountains in Florida. A ridge runs through much of the central part of the state. High points are at a hill called Iron Mountain (325 feet/99 meters) near Lake Wales, and at the highest point in the state, 345 feet (105 meters), near Lakewood.

To the east, west, and south is the coastal plain, "9,000 miles (14,484 kilometers) of detailed tidal shoreline," a generally narrow strip of land which widens in the south to take in practically all of the Everglades.

The east coast is shielded from the Atlantic by an almost continual strip of long, slim islands. Largest and longest of these is Key Largo, extending for thirty miles (48 kilometers). It is one of the necklace of islands known throughout the world as the Florida Keys. Fifty million years ago these small islands first appeared when the surface of the ocean lowered. As the ocean depths have changed, the Keys have disappeared and reappeared. The Keys nearest to the mainland are of much the same formation as the peninsula itself. Their basic material is oolite, a kind of limestone. The further Keys have been built principally by the growth of coral. The John Pennekamp coral reef off Key Largo is the only living coral reef in North American waters. On the gulf side of the Keys, the water is shallow and takes on many different vivid colors.

Although Key West is the most remote of the Keys having a permanent population, the Florida Keys actually extend much farther west to include groups called the Marquesas Keys and the remote, forbidding Dry Tortugas.

Many islands also dot the gulf coast of Florida. These include the Ten Thousand Islands west of Everglades. This tropical island group has been called "America's answer to a south sea paradise."

Some other gulf islands are Sanibel, Captiva, Lacosta, Gasparilla, Longboat Key, Cedar Key, Dog Island, St. George, St. Vincent, and Santa Rosa.

The Suwannee River is only one of Florida's 166 rivers.

Prehistoric Indian mound at Crystal River.

Footsteps on the Land

THE FIRST PEOPLE

We have a record of Florida history for a longer period of time than for any other part of the United States. Yet there may have been men and women living in the area 15,000 years before our records begin.

The exact time the first human beings came to Florida is not clear. Our only information comes from the things these early people left behind them, and Florida's climate is very poor for preserving such remains.

The earliest of these prehistoric people lived as hunters. They probably killed even huge mastodons with their pointed throwing sticks, called *atlatls*. They had no permanent villages, though they may have put up rough dwellings such as huts with palmetto thatched roofs or tepees made of wooden poles and deerskins.

Since they did not know how to make pottery, they cooked their food by roasting it over open fires or boiling it in water-filled skin bags into which they had put red-hot stones.

Later people learned the use of the bow and arrow and made crude pottery. Some of this earthenware was made inside a mold of palmetto leaves and then baked. Other clay ware was made by reinforcing the clay with Spanish moss, forming a utensil, and then baking it.

These early people ate great quantities of shellfish and tossed the shells near their homes. Some of the mounds of shells formed in this way were enormous and may still be seen in various places. Pieces of pottery and other items made by the Indians also found their way into these huge garbage heaps, and the remains help us to know how they lived. One of the outstanding mounds of this type is Turtle Mound at New Smyrna Beach.

Many of these mounds had been dug up and hauled away for road building material before the archeologists could study their contents.

Other mounds were built by ancient peoples to bury their dead or to form the base for temples or religious buildings. One of these temple mounds is found in the heart of present-day Fort Walton Beach. It is considered the largest work of ancient man on the gulf coast. It is similar to the mounds of Mayan people of the Yucatan Peninsula of Mexico. Another of these is Madira Bickel Mound, now a historical memorial.

It is not clear whether the people of Florida had contact with the Mayan or Aztec peoples, but there were well-established trade routes from Florida to the north, even as far north as present-day Ohio.

Later prehistoric people learned to grow corn and vegetables. This agricultural development made possible larger villages and a more settled way of life.

In the Florida Keys the first people, called the Arawaks, may have come by boat, gradually moving farther and farther across the Caribbean from their original home on the north coast of South America. They probably arrived in the Keys between A.D. 400 and A.D. 300.

EARLY INDIANS

When Europeans first reached Florida, they found four major Indian groups living there. The Tegesta occupied the lower east coast and the Calusa the lower west coast. The Timucua lived north of the Tegesta and the Calusa, and the Apalache lived in the gulf region west of the Aucilla River.

Estimates of the number of Indians in Florida when Europeans first came range from 5,000 to 10,000. Some experts feel there may have been a great many more than that.

The Indians of Florida had a reputation for being especially fierce. Some were supposed to have been cannibals. The Calusa attacked European explorers on sight. They made slaves of their captives and practiced human sacrifice.

Less hostile were the Timucua. They developed farming, with corn as the main crop.

One party of explorers found a fine Indian temple. Inside, it was decorated with twelve carved wooden statues of men with fierce

16

expressions. Each figure brandished a club. Six stood on each side to guard the door. The figures were wrapped in mantles of dyed skins. Their bows and quivers were decorated with feathers, copper tips, and tassels.

When chiefs traveled they sometimes went by sedan chair, carried by four bearers, with four reserve bearers waiting to take their places. Ahead of the procession went flute players to announce the great man's coming.

Today the early Indians are gone, though memory of Indian influence lingers on in many of the names of Florida. Miami was the Indian name for "big water." Ocala simply means "spring." Caloosahatchee is the "River of the Calusas," Apalachicola, "place of the ruling people," Palatka, "ferry crossing," Hialeah, "prairie," and Homosassa, "place of peppers."

JUAN PONCE DE LEÓN

Juan Ponce de León, the first recorded discoverer of Florida, sighted that peninsula on March 27, 1513. However, it is almost certain that Europeans had at least sighted it, if not set foot on it, even as early as 1497, just five years after Columbus's first voyage. Columbus himself came close to discovering the mainland near Cape Canaveral (formerly Cape Kennedy), but he missed it.

As early as 1502 Alberto Cantino made a map which clearly shows the outline of Florida. This apparently was based on the work of a Portuguese explorer who must have sailed almost around the peninsula to provide the details included on the map. Unfortunately, the name of this bold navigator of Portugal is not known to us.

Ponce de León was apparently not aware of these discoveries. But he had heard of an island where there was a wonderful fountain, said to have the power of giving eternal youth to those fortunate enough to bathe in it.

Ponce de León had come to the New World on Columbus's second voyage. He had been a Spanish administrator in Haiti and Puerto Rico and became very wealthy.

Ponce de León received permission from his monarch to seek the land of the wonderful fountain and paid all of his own expenses for three ships, crews, and provisions. He had with him a slave woman from the Bahamas who claimed to know the location of the Fountain of Youth.

Ponce de León's expedition first sighted what they thought was the island of the fountain on Easter Sunday. Consequently, they called the "island" Pascua Florida in honor of the Easter Festival of the Flowers. About April 2, Ponce de León landed on the mainland. There is no record of the exact place, but it is thought to be at or near where St. Augustine is now located.

There may have been a picturesque ceremony as the explorer took possession of the land in the name of the Spanish king. He spent several days on the mainland without any success in finding his miraculous fountain.

Resuming the voyage, he went down the coast where the currents off a certain cape caused him to name it Cape of the Currents. It later became famous as Cape Canaveral.

On this first expedition Ponce de León reached as far as a group of islands which he discovered and named the Dry Tortugas (turtles). He gave them this name because of the tremendous number of turtles found there. The men captured enough of the turtles and their eggs to add greatly to their supplies of fresh food.

Near the Ten Thousand Islands the Indians were thrown into great panic at the sight of Ponce de León's men coming out of their ships, which they thought were huge fish. But the Indians were not terrified for long; they made a savage attack on the men who went ashore for wood and water. This may have been the first battle between Indians and Europeans in what is now the United States.

Ponce de León never knew that the land he discovered was not an island. However, it was only six years later, in 1519, that Alonzo Alvarez de Pineda traced the course of the land to the point where he became convinced that it must be a part of a very large continent.

When Ponce de León returned to Florida in 1521, this time to attempt a settlement on the west coast, near present-day Charlotte Harbor, he and his men were attacked at once by the Indians and

Depiction of an Indian Village at the History Museum, Pensacola.

Ponce de León was severely wounded in spite of his armor. He was carried to his ship, and twice tried to rejoin the battle, but was not able to do so. He died shortly afterward in Cuba at the age of sixty-one. His body was returned to Puerto Rico, where he was buried.

NARVÁEZ; DE SOTO; DISASTERS

In 1528 Panfilo de Narváez sailed into Tampa Bay with a great force of two ships, four hundred men, and eighty horses. On an expedition into the interior Narváez and a force of men became separated from the ships. They tried to build new boats, turning their jewelry into tools. They even made nails from stirrup irons. They wove rope from the manes and tails of their horses, which they had been forced to eat to avoid starvation. Using their shirts for sails, they started out, but storms and other disasters overtook them.

Only four of Narváez's men ever reached civilization again. These four made one of the great marches of history, suffering great hardships as they traversed almost the entire continent.

By this time the whole east coast of North America from Mexico to Labrador was called Florida by the Spaniards.

19

Figures representing Ponce de León (1460-1521) and Hernando De Soto (1500-1542). Potter's Wax Museum, St. Augustine.

An even greater expedition than that of Narváez's was organized by wealthy, aristocratic Hernando De Soto. He was a commanding figure and liked to dramatize himself by dressing entirely in white. De Soto's army consisted of seven large and three small ships and 570 men, together with 223 horses, 300 hogs, and other livestock.

On May 30, 1539, De Soto landed for the first time near the present-day city of Tampa. He went ashore with a mighty flourish, heralded by silver trumpets and banners, his men carrying spears and dressed in glittering armor. This show of force so alarmed the Indians that they disappeared for a long time. De Soto occupied the chief's house, and his officers used other houses they found in the Indian village.

The explorer wrote to the king of Spain, giving details of his landings. This is generally considered to be the first letter ever written in what is now the United States.

De Soto was able to rescue Juan Ortiz, a member of the Narváez party who had been captured and tortured by the Indians. He would have been put to death, but the chief's daughter begged for his life.

They began their northward march of discovery, always hoping to find a great wealth of gold and jewels as the explorers of Mexico and Peru had done. They rediscovered the Bay of Horses and found Pensacola Bay. The former was the spot where Narváez and his men had been forced to eat their unfortunate mounts.

Almost no gold was found, but occasionally their hopes were raised by finding a few pearls.

During the winter they spent in the region of present-day Tallahassee, De Soto and his men observed the first Christmas (1539) in what is now the United States. In the spring they left Florida to continue their explorations and did not return there.

A group of Dominican friars, led by Luis Cancer de Barbastro, attempted to set up a mission in Florida, but they were massacred by the Indians in 1549.

Then in 1559 Don Tristán de Luna's fleet of thirteen vessels landed at the site of present-day Pensacola. He brought with him the largest expedition yet to visit Florida. About 1,600 men, women, and children were going to make the first attempt at establishing a permanent colony.

Depiction of a Spanish Landing, the History Museum, Pensacola.

This grand plan was foiled by a hurricane. All but three small ships were wrecked and most of the supplies were destroyed. The settlers remained for over a year but were finally forced by privation to return to Mexico. De Luna was a broken man, his great fortune and reputation both lost in a Florida hurricane.

MASSACRE OF THE PROTESTANTS

While Spain was bringing great wealth from its many colonies in North and South America, other countries had been enviously awaiting their own chance. Pope Alexander VI had divided the New World between Spain and Portugal, but this meant little to some of the other nations of Europe.

French Protestants, called Huguenots, were anxious to find a place in the New World where they could worship freely. One of the Huguenot leaders, Jean Ribaut, received permission from the French king to establish a Protestant colony in the New World. His voyage took seventy-two days. It was the first time ships crossing the Atlantic did not stop at islands on the way.

On May 1, 1562, Ribaut discovered the St. Johns River in Florida and named it the River of May in honor of May Day. Ribaut was tremendously impressed with the country he described as "a country of rivers, havens and islands of such surpassing fruitfulness as cannot by the tongue be expressed."

Ribaut had brought along a carved marble monument to plant in the soil of Florida to claim the land in the name of King Charles IX of France. This shaft, with the king's arms engraved on it, was beautifully made. Ribaut set up the shaft amid the palmettos of the Florida coast, and later the Indians worshipped it as an emblem of the gods.

Ribaut did not make a settlement in Florida, but he did leave thirty of his men at Port Royal Sound in what is now South Carolina.

Two years after the Ribaut expedition, one of his men, René de Laudonnière, returned to Florida with three ships and a crowd of Huguenots for settlement. They found Ribaut's monument, still

Carved marble monument set up at Fort Caroline by Jean Ribaut in 1542 to claim the land in the name of the French king.

decorated with flowers by the Indians. They built Fort Caroline five miles (eight kilometers) from the mouth of the St. Johns River, but they knew nothing about agriculture, and when their supplies ran out the Indians refused to feed them. When an English captain, Sir John Hawkins, stopped at Fort Caroline for water in August of 1565, he found the French eating anything they could find, including rattlesnakes and acorns. Hawkins offered to take the French colonists home, but they refused.

Spain, meanwhile, had been horrified that Protestants were attempting to take away her rights in Florida. She hurriedly sent one of her great leaders, Pedro Menéndez de Avilés, to drive the intruders out and restore the land to Spanish control.

At about the same time, Ribaut was hurrying to rescue his French colony. Ribaut and Menéndez, with their fleets and armies, arrived in Florida at almost exactly the same hour.

Menéndez had used his own money, over two million dollars, to bring his expedition to Florida. Menéndez found himself in a harbor that he called St. Augustine because it was that saint's day. It has kept that name ever since. With elaborate ceremonies he took possession in the name of the Spanish king. He hurried to erect a fort at St. Augustine in fear of an attack by Ribaut. St. Augustine has been occupied continuously ever since that September, and is the oldest continuing settlement in the United States.

Meanwhile Ribaut, with a large fleet, five hundred men, women, and children, and provisions, had landed at Fort Caroline. The starving French settlers rejoiced. Ribaut knew that only a part of Menéndez's fleet had arrived, so he hurriedly sailed from Fort Caroline to attack St. Augustine before Menéndez's reinforcements could arrive.

Here again a hurricane, the worst storm in the memory of the Indians, swept Ribaut away from his attack; along with most of his men, he was shipwrecked on an island.

Taking advantage of Ribaut's absence, Menéndez attacked Fort Caroline by land. Most of the Frenchmen were killed. Only a few, including Laudonnière, escaped and finally made their way back to Europe. Another of those who escaped was the young artist Jacques le Moyne, who had drawn the plans for Fort Caroline. Le Moyne, the first professional artist in America, had drawn many pictures of the Indians and of life in Florida. He published a book of these pictures, telling of his experiences. This has become one of the most famous and informative books in the history of literature. Le Moyne's drawings are still used today to illustrate conditions in Florida during that period.

Next Menéndez set out to find the remnants of Ribaut's forces. Within two weeks, 330 French Protestants had surrendered. Menéndez had them bound and beheaded without mercy, including Ribaut, not because they were enemies but because they refused to accept Catholicism. The spot has been named Matanzas, or "slaughter," ever since.

Three years later, another Frenchman, Dominique de Gourgues, swept down on Fort Caroline, which had been renamed San Mateo. With the help of friendly Indians, all the Spaniards at San Mateo were either killed in battle or hanged in revenge for his countrymen. He also wanted revenge on the Spanish for his own mistreatment as a Spanish galley slave.

Menéndez and his successors were unable to do much to strengthen the settlements in Florida. In 1586 Sir Francis Drake, an Englishman, captured St. Augustine and burned it to the ground. The Spaniards, however, rebuilt the town.

MISSIONS

In 1592, twelve Franciscan monks arrived in St. Augustine to set up a series of missions. One of these was on what is now Fort George Island. By 1597 there were twenty missions in Florida, an almost incredible accomplishment in five years' time. At the height of their success these self-sacrificing men of God operated two chains of missions, one stretching northward from St. Augustine for two hundred miles (322 kilometers), the other as far as the Apalachicola River. Unfortunately, these missions have not survived, as have some California missions.

Just as the sixteenth century drew to a close, there occurred an event which brings a light to most people's eyes even today. The first great Spanish treasure ship ever to be sunk in those waters, the *Santa Margarita,* went down on a hidden reef at a point about halfway between Jupiter and Palm Beach. More than six million dollars' worth of treasure disappeared with her beneath the waves.

For almost a hundred years life in Florida moved on without especially outstanding events. Governors came and went; priests and friars taught the Indians; pirates attacked and plundered. Spanish settlement was lightly sprinkled throughout much of northern Florida.

UNDER MANY FLAGS

As the 1600s came to an end the Spanish hurried to make a major settlement on the gulf coast in what is now the panhandle. Pensacola was begun and fortified in 1698. This was not a moment too soon for the Spanish, for a French force arrived, ready to settle in the same place. Finding the Spanish too strong, the French finally went elsewhere.

From 1700 to 1763 Florida was bandied back and forth as the great countries of Europe fought with one another and brought their wars to their colonies. In 1702 English settlers from South Carolina captured Saint Augustine, but were not able to overcome Castillo de

Castillo de San Marcos, the fort begun by the Spanish in 1672.

San Marcos, the great old fortress that had been begun in 1672. The English finally withdrew.

In 1719 the French captured Pensacola. That city changed hands four times within the course of a single year.

When Spain and England went to war in 1739, Governor Oglethorpe of Georgia prepared to attack Spanish Florida. Most of the Indians lined up with one or the other of the rival sides. In 1740 and 1742 Oglethorpe and his Indian allies attacked St. Augustine without much success. The war between England and Spain lasted for many years and cost millions of dollars. It was called the War of Jenkin's Ear, and came about because the Spanish had cut off the ear of an English captain.

In 1750 England and Spain again went to war. The British captured Spain's greatest possession in the New World—Havana. In order to get Havana back at the end of the war, the Spanish traded Florida for it. So in 1763 Florida was added to the other British colonies in America. Most of the Spanish settlers with any property left Florida before the British came.

When the British took over, they found little to show for the 250 years Florida had been in Spanish hands. There were two tiny towns, St. Augustine in east Florida, and Pensacola in west Florida. The British divided the area into separate colonies of East and West Florida, and made the two towns capital of each. There was only one other settlement—St. Marks. The rest had again become wilderness.

The wars and Indian troubles had swept away the wonderful missions. Roads and trails had become overgrown. Only six hundred Europeans remained in all of Florida.

In the period from 1763 to 1783, when the British ruled Florida, more improvements were made in the area than during the whole 250 years of Spanish rule. Settlement was promoted, treaties were made with the Indians for their land, surveys were carried out, and land grants were made, some as large as 20,000 acres (8,094 hectares). Trade was carried on, particularly with the Indians.

When the colonies to the north declared their independence from England and the Revolutionary War began, Florida remained loyal to the mother country. In fact, the few citizens who lived there were so loyal that the American patriots John Adams and John Hancock were burned in effigy in St. Augustine's public park. Castillo de San Marcos housed a number of American prisoners during the Revolution. Then as the Revolution continued to succeed, many loyalists from the embattled colonies fled to safety in Florida.

When Spain entered the war against England, the Spanish quickly captured Pensacola and gained the whole territory of West Florida. This included a great deal more land than it does today.

The Revolution was barely over when England again made an exchange—this time Florida for the Bahamas and Gibraltar, and Florida became Spanish again.

During this period of their rule, the Spanish had little more success than before. Most of the British settlers moved away. The flourishing agriculture of the British period came almost to a halt. Pirates plundered and illegal trade with the Indians flourished. American settlers kept pushing into the territory. In fact, in 1812, American settlers in East Florida declared their independence from Spain and tried to set up a Republic of East Florida. They were not successful, though the "Republic" actually was in existence for almost three years.

In the War of 1812 between the United States and England, a naval battle was fought off the coast of Cape Canaveral in 1814. On November 6, 1814, General Andrew Jackson captured Pensacola, because the Spanish had permitted British troops to come in. The general was very careful of the rights of the residents there; he told them if he had done any damage, to put in their claims. More than a hundred years later, in 1931, the United States did pay Spain damages for Jackson's campaign in Spanish Pensacola.

It is generally known that the last great battle of the War of 1812, Andrew Jackson at New Orleans, was actually fought after the peace treaty had been signed. It is not so well known that the War of 1812 continued even after that in Florida, and the last action of the war was carried out by the British on Cumberland Island, where they finally heard about the peace treaty.

Disorder continued in Florida. General Gregor MacGregor captured Amelia Island in 1817. He hoped to get American aid to take the territory away from Spain. When this failed he turned the affair over to his lieutenant, Jared Irwin, who withstood a Spanish attack. Irwin was succeeded by the pirate Luis Aury. Aury raised the Mexican flag and declared that Amelia Island had been annexed to Mexico. United States troops finally took possession of Amelia Island, just to keep order, when it became clear that Spain could not do so.

General Andrew Jackson, who was in Florida during the War of 1812, also became the first American governor of Florida.

Once again, in 1818, Andrew Jackson moved with troops into Florida. This time he came to rid the area of Indians and others who had been making trouble for American settlers. During what is called the First Seminole War (1817-1818), Jackson captured and hanged two British citizens who had been accused of inciting the Indians against the Americans. At the Miccosuckee Indian village, Jackson found three hundred scalps of men, women, and children on painted war poles over the village square.

When Jackson again took Pensacola, the United States was in actual possession of all of West Florida. Jackson retained Pensacola until the arrival of a Spanish force that was able to keep the peace.

On February 22, 1819, Spain signed a treaty ceding Florida to the United States, but this was not ratified by Spain until 1821. The United States agreed to pay Spain up to five million dollars for claims of Florida residents. Actually no money changed hands but a story circulated that the ship transporting the money to Spain was sunk, probably in the neighborhood of the mouth of the Suwanee River. Another tale of Florida's many sunken treasures had come into being. This treasure has been sought without success ever since.

THE STARS AND STRIPES

General Jackson was once again in Pensacola on July 17, 1821, to receive the formal transfer of West Florida to the United States. His party passed between rows of Spanish and American soldiers to the Government House, where as Jackson himself said, "his Catholic majesty's flag was lowered, and the American hoisted high in the air, not less than a hundred feet," while a military band played.

East Florida had already been transferred, and the American flag flew at last over Castillo de San Marcos, which had never been captured in battle.

As first American governor of Florida, Andrew Jackson began the job of organizing his area, but he soon resigned and Congress created the Territory of Florida, with William P. Duval as the first territorial governor.

At this time the only communities of any size in Florida were St. Augustine and Pensacola, separated by 400 miles (644 kilometers) of jungle and several thousand Indians. In order for the St. Augustine members of the territorial legislature to meet in Pensacola, they had to travel around the peninsula by ship. When they went to the first meeting, their two ships were wrecked and one legislator was drowned.

Because it was more centrally located, Tallahassee was selected in 1823 to be the capital. The first meeting of the legislature at Tallahassee took place in 1824 in a log cabin built for the purpose.

One of the most needed improvements in Florida came in 1825 and 1826 when a road was opened from St. Augustine to Pensacola, by way of Tallahassee. Another great aid to transportation was the coming of the steamboat. The first steamboat operated on the Apalachicola River as early as 1827.

THE SECOND SEMINOLE WAR

During the term of Governor Duval, Florida had known a period of expansion and comparative peace with the Indians. The Indians feared and respected Governor Duval. At one time he had seized fierce Chief Neamathla by the throat in the presence of three hundred of his warriors. By this action the governor had persuaded the chief to accept his point of view.

By 1834, however, the Indians were growing restless. These were not any of the groups of Indians found by the original explorers more than three hundred years before. Almost none of the original groups were left in Florida. Gradually during the late 1700s more and more Creek Indians had come to Florida from the north. They eventually were called the Seminoles. In 1823 at the Treaty of Moultrie Creek, the Seminoles had agreed to move south, to the central part of the peninsula. In 1832, at the Treaty of Paynes Landing, the Indians agreed to leave Florida entirely and to be moved to the West. Although the Indians were reluctant to go, the government set a deadline of January 1, 1836, for the move.

Indian leader Osceola (left)
as painted by George Catlin
and Chief Billy Bowlegs (above)
as painted by Charles Bird King.

Just before the deadline Osceola, who was not a chief but was a great Indian leader, killed the Indian agent, General Wiley Thompson, near Ocala.

At about the same time Major Francis L. Dade was surprised by an Indian war party. Major Dade and most of his company of 139 men were killed. One soldier, named Thomas, almost suffocated under the dead bodies of his comrades but was rescued by an Indian who knew him and who, for payment of six dollars, let him escape. Two or three others pulled themselves from the slaughtered bodies and escaped.

The seven-year war with the Seminoles which followed has been called the most costly Indian war in United States history. The number of troops sent to conquer the Indians was greater than had ever before been assembled in Florida for any one cause. The financial cost is estimated at twenty million dollars.

Among the famous army men who took part in the war were Zachary Taylor and William Tecumseh Sherman. Colonel Taylor, who later became both a famed general and president, commanded the

31

troops from 1838 to 1840. Sherman, who had just graduated from West Point, was stationed at Fort Pierce. It is ironic that Sherman's middle name, "Tecumseh," was that of one of America's most famous Indians, and his first assignment was to fight the Indians.

The Indians were elusive, and it was almost impossible to bring them into battle. After Osceola was finally captured, Chief Coacoochee continued the fight until he himself was captured in 1841. When Coacoochee agreed to be resettled, other chiefs began to agree, also.

Only Chiefs Billy Bowlegs and Sam Jones refused to surrender. Finally, the United States agreed to give them a reservation in the Everglades area and the fighting came to an end. It was estimated that about three hundred Seminoles remained in Florida.

Although most new settlement in Florida had been stopped by the Second Seminole War, the army had been able during its marches to complete most of the exploration of the state. By the time the Second Seminole War was over, most of the state had been mapped.

TWENTY-SEVENTH STATE

In 1839, during the Second Seminole War, Florida had adopted a constitution. An interesting clause proposed in this constitution would have kept any man from holding public office if he were a "dueler, bank director or minister of the gospel." Fortunately, this part of the constitution was not adopted. When Florida applied for statehood, Congress failed to act immediately on the application because those who were opposed to slavery did not want another slave state.

Finally, Iowa was about ready to become a state; this would provide another free state to balance Florida as a slave state. So on March 3, 1845, President John Tyler signed the bill making Florida a state. This was the last day of his term as president and one of his last official acts. William D. Moseley became the first governor. David Levy, who later changed his name to Yulee, and James D. Westcott were Florida's first United States senators.

32

Yesterday and Today

WAR BETWEEN THE STATES

In the period after the Second Seminole War, Florida grew rapidly and prospered.

Many of the soldiers who had served in the Second Seminole War were given "scrip," papers that could be exchanged for title to Florida land. A number of soldiers took advantage of this.

The greatest acreage of cultivation in Florida was that of the huge plantations where cotton and sugarcane were grown. No accurate record remains today of how much land was occupied by these mammoth plantations with their beautiful southern mansions and their thousands of slaves. The plantation system depended entirely on slave labor.

When the disagreements between the North and South over slavery finally led to war, Florida, in agreement with her southern neighbors, voted to secede from the Union on January 10, 1861. The state joined the newly formed Confederate States of America on April 22.

Kingsley Plantation State Park is a reminder of Florida's plantation days.

When war came, most people in both the North and South expected it to last only two or three months. Although the war dragged on for four years, there was probably less actual fighting on Florida soil than in any of the other Southern states, though Florida troops served in all major battles in other states. In Florida the first shots of the war were fired at Fort Pickens.

More than fifteen thousand Florida men saw service in the war. Because of the state's small population, this must have included almost every man of military age in the state during the whole period of the war.

The principal aim of the Union forces in Florida was to keep the state's great supplies of food and provisions from reaching the Confederate fighting front and to maintain a blockade to keep other countries from trading along the Florida coast. Much of the Florida coast was controlled by Union forces. Jacksonville was occupied on four different occasions by Union troops.

In spite of their efforts, Union forces were unable to prevent many goods from being run through the coastal blockade. Cotton, tobacco, and turpentine went out; medicine, munitions, and other goods came in. Florida provided much needed salt to the Confederacy through many factories that boiled the salt from ocean water. Toward the end of the war, Florida cattle herds were about the only source of beef for the Confederacy. Grains, sugar, fish, and hogs from Florida also played an important part in feeding the people.

Union authorities finally decided to seal off these supplies from Florida. More than five thousand Union troops met a Confederate force at Olustee on February 20, 1864, in the largest battle of the war on Florida soil. This battle became a great Confederate victory, with over eighteen hundred Union troops killed, missing, or wounded. From this time on, Union forces did not reach very far into the interior of Florida, but were kept to the coastal points they had already occupied. Fort Pickens at Pensacola, Fort Taylor at Key West, and Fort Jefferson on the Dry Tortugas were the only forts the Confederate forces were never able to seize. More ships were stationed at Key West than at any other place along the Atlantic Coast, and Key West is credited with a major role in the Northern victory.

Toward the end of the war a Union force landed at St. Marks, apparently intending to capture Tallahassee. All available men rushed to defend the capital. Old men and cadets from the West Florida Seminary and a mixed group of others took part in the Battle of Natural Bridge on March 6, 1865.

"From boys of fourteen to men of seventy, from the humble woodsmen to the highest civil dignitaries, all came to the defense of their country," according to General William Miller who commanded the Confederate troops.

When General Miller heard that his men were thinking of abandoning the fort at St. Marks, he went there immediately and said, "This fort is to be defended. The troops at Newport and the Natural Bridge stand between you and the enemy. You cannot be attacked from the rear and if you are assailed in front, with your gun trained on the river, you can sink every boat. I will hear no more of the abandonment of this strong position, and I will hold him a traitor who speaks again of the abandonment of this position, the key to the defense of Tallahassee."

The defenders were successful, and Union forces never took Tallahassee. This was the only Confederate capital east of the Mississippi that was not captured.

However, when the war came to an end, the Stars and Stripes were again raised over Tallahassee on May 20, 1865.

A thousand Florida troops had been killed in action and another five thousand had died of disease and suffering. Five thousand more were wounded. Fewer than five thousand of all Florida's troops escaped being killed, being wounded, or dying in service. The state is said to have had the largest percentage of its population in Civil War service of any state.

Several members of the Confederate cabinet and other high ranking Confederate figures were able to escape to Florida. Judah P. Benjamin, who was called the "brains of the Confederacy," disguised himself as a black cook and fled from Sarasota by boat to Havana. John C. Breckinridge, Confederate secretary of war, and several others captured a small boat near Lake Worth and sailed to safety in Havana.

A TIME OF TRIAL

When Florida refused to ratify the Fourteenth Amendment, the state came under military rule. Florida had no representation in the thirty-seventh, thirty-eighth, and thirty-ninth sessions of the Congress of the United States. Then with a new constitution and ratification of the Fourteenth Amendment, in 1868, Congress again recognized Florida as a state of the Union.

The former way of life was gone in Florida. Most of the wealth had vanished. Some plantations were divided into small farms but most of them simply went out of cultivation. Bitterness and disputes among black and white, between Southerner and Northerner, made disruption continual. Gradually, however, order was restored. By 1877 all federal troops were withdrawn from Florida.

JUST WHAT IS A SWAMP?

In the western states most public land was owned by the United States government. Under the Homestead Act, individuals were allowed to claim a limited amount of land for their own use. In Florida, however, a large part of the public land had passed to the state under the Swamp Land Act. This act gave every state all swamp and overflowed land within its borders.

Instead of realizing a profit on these lands, by the 1870s the state was in debt and had little prospect of finding money to pay the debt. Then in 1881 a wealthy Philadelphia saw manufacturer, Hamilton Disston, agreed to pay the state a million dollars for 4 million acres (1.6 million hectares) of state land. This paved the way for opening much of Florida for development.

QUAKE, FREEZE, NEW LIFE

In 1885 Florida adopted a more democratic constitution and gave the people a greater share in their government. In 1886 the state

Mangrove Swamp, Marianna

experienced the first and only earthquake ever known there. The shock rang St. Augustine's bells and caused a mild panic. Another kind of natural disaster ended in 1888 with the last of the great yellow fever epidemics.

In 1893 a unique group of settlers came to Florida and began to carve out a new home in the wilderness. Most of the settlers were from Chicago, and were the followers of Dr. Cyrus R. Teed, who called himself Koresh. His cult was called Koreshan Unity.

Though they had no prior knowledge of building, the Koreshans managed to construct picturesque houses, an art gallery, a bakery, and a saw mill. Their village, called Estero, was forty miles (sixty-four kilometers) from the nearest railroad. They had symphony concerts, published books, and enjoyed baseball and water sports.

The basis of their belief was the unity of religion and science, but their scientific beliefs were somewhat eccentric. They taught that mankind actually lived on the inside of the earth, with all life on its inner surface.

Because they did not marry, the Koreshans diminished in numbers until in 1961 there were only four remaining. These four voted to turn their properties over to the state, and today visitors to the 305-acre (123-hectare) tract may see the quaint and historic village of Estero almost as it was in its best period.

Another scientific interest of the Koreshans was horticulture. They brought exotic plant life from tropical countries all over the globe, making this an outstanding horticultural region.

In 1894 and 1895, the most severe freeze in Florida history almost destroyed the state's agriculture. Practically every orange tree in the state was affected.

With the coming of the Spanish-American War in 1898, human rather than natural destruction next claimed Florida's attention. Before the war began, arms and supplies had been illegally transported from secret bases in Florida to patriots who wanted to overthrow the Spanish government in Cuba. One of the leaders in these risky voyages was Captain Napoleon Bonaparte Broward, who later became governor of Florida and was elected a United States senator. Many of the patriots were able to escape to Florida, where large numbers of them found refuge at Jacksonville.

When the United States battleship *Maine* was sunk in Havana Harbor and war came, Florida was the main point of embarkation for troops and supplies, with the centers at Tampa, Jacksonville, and Miami. Tampa served as the principal port for troop movement. Theodore Roosevelt drilled his Rough Riders in the backyard of the Tampa Bay Hotel.

The war money spent there and the activities during the war brought new life to Florida. Many of the servicemen who had become familiar with the state either came back for vacations or settled there permanently.

REAL ESTATE IN ORBIT

On May 3, 1901, Jacksonville was almost completely wiped out by fire. By the time the fire was put out, 466 acres (188 hectares) of the older part of the city lay in smoking ruins. However, it was not long before a better city was rising from the ashes.

The building of railroads was one of the important activities of this period. H. M. Flagler's railroad reached Miami in 1896. Then Mr. Flagler had an idea that most people considered completely ridiculous. He decided to build his railroad over the sea a hundred miles (161 kilometers) farther, all the way to Key West. The building of a railroad over the sea, touching the Keys as it went, is one of the remarkable engineering accomplishments of all time. The first train reached Key West in 1912.

The Maine saluting the Spanish Flagship on arriving in Havana Harbor, *painting by H. Reuterdahl.*

During World War I Florida was particularly suited to the training of pilots because of its year-round good weather, and the state quickly took a lead in aviation which it has kept to the present time. In this war Florida people more than did their part, both at home and on the fighting fronts.

Not long after the war was over, the state began to experience one of the most remarkable periods in its history. Florida real estate, of course, had always been of interest to those who wanted to make money, but what happened, beginning in about 1919, was incredible.

In that year Carl Fisher scooped sand from Biscayne Bay to create an island where previously there had been only swampland. He built a four-mile-long (six kilometers) wooden bridge connecting the island to the mainland and advertised his unknown island of Miami Beach with a tremendous campaign. All over Florida other promoters began to follow his lead.

Nearby Coral Gables was founded by George E. Merrick. An island appeared in Tampa Bay, coaxed over the surface of the water by D. P. Davis, who called it Davis Island.

Promoters began to bring prospects by the busload from as far as New York and Chicago. People flocked to these new-found paradises.

When the Flagler railroad first reached Miami, the community had a population of 60. By 1920 the population was 30,000; four years later it had more than doubled; in another ten years there were 200,000 people in Miami. When all available land in the Miami area had been spoken for, plans quickly were made to dredge more islands out of the bays. Lots were sold for $25,000 on land which had not yet appeared out of the bay. Although hundreds of extra clerks were hired, they were several months behind in recording Miami area land titles.

So much building was going on all over the state that supplies could not be brought in fast enough and manufacturers could not keep up with the demand. The ancient Truxillo Cathedral in Honduras made some needed money by selling its wonderful roofing tiles. The cathedral roof was covered with galvanized iron, while Miami roofs were graced with coverings from an ancient cathedral.

William Jennings Bryan said that Miami was the only place in the world where a man could tell a lie at breakfast that would come true before nightfall. New towns were laid out. Roads, sewers, schools, and street lighting were put in. Speculators bought property on credit; when customers failed to buy up the land available, many speculators failed. The bubble burst. Before the state could begin to recover, the depression of 1929 had set in, and Florida was the first state to feel the worst effects of this depression.

The seriousness of the situation is illustrated by the fact that in 1925 Florida's state banks had deposits of 466 million dollars. By 1930 deposits had shrunk to 59 million.

In this first great land boom, millions of dollars were written off as a total loss; towns were left half-built and unoccupied. In some places block after block of street signs were the only reminders of cities that never came into being. On the other hand, many permanent improvements greatly benefited the state, and as someone said, "the sun continued to shine."

One of the most lasting accomplishments of the boom years ranks with the railroad to Key West as an engineering achievement. For more than four hundred years the Everglades were assumed to be impenetrable. Then in 1928 a road connecting Tampa and Miami was completed. It cut straight across the Everglades. The road was named the Tamiami Trail. Building it demanded the invention of entirely new types of huge roadbuilding equipment, some of which is still in use today.

In 1926 the collapse of the boom in Miami was hurried by one of the worst hurricanes ever to strike there. The city experienced sixteen hours of destruction. When the eye of the hurricane passed over, the air became so rare that hundreds fainted for lack of oxygen. The barometer reading was the lowest ever recorded in the United States. At Miami Beach a tidal wave greatly added to the damage. More than two hundred people were dead in the Miami area, and the disaster cost a billion dollars over the state as a whole.

In 1933 tragedy of a different kind came to Miami. President-elect Franklin D. Roosevelt was riding in a car with Mayor Anton Cermak of Chicago. An assassin attempted to kill Roosevelt, but fatally wounded Mayor Cermak instead. The killer, Guiseppi Zangara, was electrocuted in Raiford Prison for the crime.

World War II transformed Florida into one of the great military training and transportation centers of all time. On the east coast alone there were more than thirty training installations. Both coasts offered intensive training for the invasions of Pacific shores as well as North Africa and Europe. Key West had a sonar school and Miami a Submarine Chaser Training Center. The Tokyo raiders of General Doolittle trained at Eglin Field. Florida was the key to the African airlift during the war.

THE ROCKETS' RED GLARE

Little attention was paid when the government set up a rocket station at Cape Canaveral. Scant notice was given the flight of the first rocket launched from Canaveral in 1950. The United States still had not developed its own rocket, and the one used in 1950 was a German V-2. Only after October, 1957, when the Russians sent up their first satellite, Sputnik, did the American people show an intense interest in rockets.

The attention of the world turned to Cape Canaveral as never before when America's first satellite, Explorer I, was launched from there.

Launch of the Saturn Space Vehicle used in the Apollo Space Program to place a man on the moon. (NASA)

A rocket at takeoff, Cape Canaveral, Florida.

In 1961 an American rode a rocket for the first time when Astronaut Alan Shepherd took off from Florida's famous cape on a suborbital flight. Then the world watched, scarcely daring to breathe, as Commander John Glenn climbed confidently into his Friendship VII capsule and became the first American in orbit. From the land where early explorers struggled to travel a few miles a day, a modern man took off to circle the globe in little more than an hour. Now one of the most incredible accomplishments of mankind has become almost commonplace in Florida.

Since that first flight, all of America's spacemen have taken off from Florida soil.

A PROBLEM WITH A BEARD

For more than four hundred years Florida had close relations with its neighbor Cuba. When a bearded dictator, Fidel Castro, set himself up over the people of Cuba and declared that he was a communist, the friendship of centuries was broken off.

Thousands of Cubans fled and found refuge in Florida, particularly in the Miami region. Many of them had lost everything they had, often including family and friends. Florida was sympathetic to these people and their troubles, but the concentration of so many thousands of new people in a single area created extraordinary problems for the state. With the help of the United States government, these problems were eased as the months went by.

Many of these refugees organized groups in Florida aimed at recovering their country. The controversial raid by anti-Castro forces, which ended in disaster at the Bay of Pigs in Cuba, was rehearsed on Florida shores and has become one of the most discussed events in modern American history.

In October of 1962 President John F. Kennedy announced that the Russians were building a great atomic missile force in Cuba, which threatened a wide area in the United States with nuclear destruction, particularly the critical metropolitan centers of Florida.

During this crisis, Florida was the scene of one of the most extraordinary concentrations of military might in the history of the world. Vast numbers of troops, weapons, armaments, ships, planes, and supplies were airlifted into the state almost overnight, all poised to strike at Cuba, over a short span of water.

Fortunately, this show of strength and determination caused the Russians to back down, and the mighty Florida force was never needed.

Only a year later, in 1963, the president who faced that problem in Cuba was struck down by an assassin.

Florida's Kennedy Space Center on Cape Canaveral has been the nation's launching platform, with the moon flights beginning in 1969; Skylab, the first orbiting laboratory; and the 1975 joint flight with Soviet Union cosmonauts.

44

In the mid-1970s the most dramatic development has been the nearly unbelievable growth of industry and tourism and the influx of new residents who have made the state's rate of population increase the highest in the nation.

Cinderella Castle at Disney World, the huge amusement park that has greatly aided the growth of tourism in Florida.

Natural Treasures

LAND OF TREES

The soils, climate, and moisture of Florida have given it a great richness in trees, plants, and shrubs, including many that are extremely rare and exotic.

One of the most interesting trees in a land filled with interesting products of the soil is the Caribbean pine tree found in southern Florida. At about Christmas time, cones appear on the tips of the branches. Because these cones give the tree the appearance of a Christmas tree covered with candles, it has been nicknamed the "Christmas tree." The cones continue to grow, and by Easter time each cone has sprouted a cross piece, making the tree appear to be covered with Easter crosses.

Among Florida's best-known trees is the cypress. In Corkscrew Swamp south of Immokalee is found the largest stand of virgin bald cypress in the United States.

The big tree donated to the state of Florida by Senator and Mrs. M.O. Overstreet is probably the largest cypress in the United States. It stands 126 feet (38.4 meters) high, has a diameter of 17½ feet (5.3 meters) and a circumference of 47 feet (14.3 meters). It is thought to be from three thousand to thirty-five hundred years old. When this tree was presented in 1929, President Calvin Coolidge presided at the dedication, and the tree was named "The Senator" in honor of its donor.

Another notable group of Florida trees is the stand of coconut palms at Miami Beach in Crandon Park. This is the largest stand of these trees in North America.

Oddities such as the soapberry tree and the torchwood tree are to be found. The torchwood burns brightly for a much longer time than ordinary trees because of its heavy pitch. When the seeds of the

Opposite: Cypress are among the best-known of Florida's many types of trees.

soapberry tree were crushed by the early settlers, they sprinkled the pulp on the water. This stupefied the fish and made them easy to catch.

Two rare native trees are the torreya, named for Dr. John Torrey, and the even rarer Florida yew. Torreya State Park takes its name from the trees found there. The common name of the torreya is stinking cedar because of its disagreeable smell. The Florida yew, on the other hand, gives off a very pleasant odor.

Visitors who see the poinciana tree in bloom will never forget the brilliance of its blossoms and the wide expanse they cover.

Many useful trees grow in Florida in addition to those used for timber. The cabbage palm (Sabal palmetto) was one of the first to have its merit discovered. Possibly for this reason, as well as for its beauty, it was named the state tree of Florida in 1953. It has been used since earliest times for the delicious heart of palm from the white, tender top bud. This tastes more like artichoke than cabbage, but the name continues.

Mulberries, olives, guavas, avocados, and almost every other fruit or commercial tree have been grown in Florida, with varying degrees of success. Eucalyptus, though not a native, grows tremendously, sometimes reaching a height of seventy feet (21.3 meters) and a thickness of twenty inches (50.8 centimeters) in as little as six years. Florida's most famous tree, the orange, is not a native either. Wild

Florida's flame vine splashes color on homes, tree trunks, and nearly anywhere else it can climb.

oranges found in such places as Highlands Hammock State Park are thought to have grown from seed dropped by early Spanish explorers.

Sixty-four percent of Florida's land is still covered with forests. The southern yellow pines are the "life blood of its huge forest industries." In the decade between 1950 and 1960 Florida's pine forests diminished. New trees and new growth did not keep up with the trees cut or burned. The state's greatest forest need is to plant new trees and conserve the present supplies until new growth is at least equal to the demand. Fire is one of the problems, and Florida seems to have one of the worst forest fire problems in the nation.

Altogether 314 species of trees grow in Florida. More than half of all the kinds of trees found in North America north of Mexico are found in Florida.

PROFUSION OF FLOWERS

Florida lives up to its reputation as a land of flowers by producing a profusion of three thousand different varieties of flowers. Most of these are native, but many have been imported. Among these is the rare African Cycad at Fairchild Gardens. Only four of these are to be found in the United States. This is one of the oldest seed-bearing plants on earth. Its seed cone is two feet (.6 meter) tall and brilliant red in color.

Jacaranda, hibiscus, azalea, camellia, gardenia, bird of paradise, air plants, yellow jasmine, Cherokee roses, exotic foliage plants, flame vine, mimosa, oleander, poinsettia, and Spanish bayonet all flash their colors across the Florida scene in various seasons. Visitors who are accustomed to seeing small poinsettia plants in pots can scarcely recover from the sight of enormous "trees" covered with hundreds of enormous poinsettia blossoms.

Those women who cherish a corsage of a single orchid might open their eyes in astonishment to see them blooming wild and spreading blooms of pink, purple, or yellow over the piney woods, marshes, and lowlands—yellow and white fringed orchids, "earrings," spiders, butterflies, the rare ixia, like a blue iris, and dozens of other native species. One of the most interesting is the bee swarm orchid, with one stalk bearing as many as two hundred yellow and brown flowers, like a swarm of bees.

The tree orchids of southern Florida are larger and more impressive in their individual blooms, and there are more than twenty-five native varieties of these. The Orchid Jungle, south of Miami, claims to be the world's largest outdoor orchid garden, with orchid plants from every tropical country growing on huge oak trees.

The showy bougainvillea vine climbs in great profusion over trees, trellises, and sides of buildings. One vine may spread a mass of brilliant purple, flame, pink, or scarlet over an area of 200 square feet (18.6 square meters). These are featured to great advantage in the Sunken Gardens at St. Petersburg.

The rare beaded fern may be found at Gold Head Branch State Park. The resurrection fern grows on the leaning trunks of live oaks. In dry weather it shrinks into a brown dead-looking ball, but with moisture it revives into sparkling green.

More than forty of Florida's plants are used for medicinal purposes, including the pleurisy root, witch hazel, horehound, ginseng, pussy willow, sassafras, skullcap, tamarind, and prickly ash.

WILDLIFE

One of the rarest and most prized animals in America is the tiny key deer. It once was hunted mercilessly. Often one man would kill more than a dozen in a day. Sometimes grass fires were set to drive them out of hiding. At other times they were harpooned while swimming. Key deer were saved from extinction in the 1950s by conservationists, particularly the Boone and Crockett Club. Now these vanishing creatures are protected by the United States government in the Key Deer National Wildlife Refuge, created in 1957.

The great forest expanses and wide swamp and grassy areas make Florida a haven for a tremendous animal population, including the white-tail deer, bear, raccoon, opossum, panther, and many others.

Macaws and flamingos (left) can be seen in the huge aviary at Sunken Gardens. The American alligator (below), Florida's most well-known reptile, was once in danger of extinction, but is now strictly protected.

For those animals and birds that are not protected permanently, 3,200,000 acres (1,294,995 hectares) in Florida are opened to public hunting, in season.

Florida also is home to a tremendous variety of reptiles, including many lizards and snakes, among them the diamondback rattlesnake, a surprisingly strong swimmer, who travels easily from key to key.

Of course, Florida's most famous reptile is the alligator. This living fossil had been hunted for its hide until it seemed in danger of disappearing. Now these Florida "dragons" are strictly protected. For the uninitiated there are few thrills that equal sighting one of the huge alligators sunning itself on a hummock in the Everglades or finding a small one almost at your feet in one of the cultivated jungle gardens.

However, the Florida birds in fantastic variety are probably the most fascinating of all the state's wildlife.

Visitors are especially attracted to the anhinga, or water turkey. His nickname of snake bird comes from his habit of walking around on the bottom of a lagoon with only the long neck and head undulating above the water, like a snake, while he searches for food. Unlike waterfowl, the anhinga has little waterproofing on its feathers and must come out frequently to dry itself. When a number of anhingas lie in the sun together with wings outstretched to dry, they look something like a large family wash.

Another of Florida's strange birds is the rare limpkin, which feeds mostly on snails, and hobbles as it walks. Its weird call has been described as the "wail of a maniac."

The most popular and amusing bird is the pelican, seen everywhere along Florida seacoasts. The awkward clownishness of these great birds on land is changed to splendid grace as they soar in flight formation. Their skill in fishing is the envy of every fisherman who

Florida's pelicans are seen all along the seacoasts.

A sailfish gives a fisherman a real battle as it leaps out of the water after being hooked.

watches them hit the water in a tremendous power dive and come up with a prize catch. Pelican Island, established in 1903, was the first migratory bird refuge in the United States.

The beauty of Florida's swamp and wading birds is another of the state's true natural assets. The popular pink flamingos, great white herons, ibis, egrets, and roseate spoonbills, with their flat, brilliant-hued bills, all add to the color of the Florida scene. Mature egrets were slaughtered without mercy to provide decoration for ladies' hats. The young were left to starve in the nests. Egret plumes were shipped to northern hat makers by the hundreds of thousands. Now, however, the egret is strictly protected, and fortunately this beautiful bird has made a comeback.

Florida's sooty and noddy terns are the only ones found in the continental United States. As many as 100,000 sooty terns nest on Bush Key. Their nests are merely depressions in the sand. The parents take turns in shading the eggs from the hot sun.

American eagles, ospreys, turkey buzzards, man-o-war birds, and many other large birds also make Florida their home.

A fantastic number of birds also stop briefly on their annual migrations. These include beautiful white-crowned pigeons, and mourning doves in unbelievable numbers.

"With the doves come many species of hawks," according to expert Bill Ackerman. "So, too, do some of the larger wading birds, particularly the American egret. To believe it one must actually see this normally slow-flying bird with a wingspread of more than six feet (1.8 meters) knock a dove out of a flight and alight on the ground to swallow it whole—a big meal with little effort."

To many visitors, especially fishermen, Florida's most interesting natural creatures are found under the water. Florida waters are home to 1,200 species of fish plus a great variety of seafood in other categories, such as shrimp and oysters. Human oyster gatherers have to compete with the drumfish for oysters. This sturdy fish can gather and harvest an oyster as expertly as any human.

Sport fishermen turn their attention to everything from the "best black bass lake in the United States" to the big game fishing of the Florida coasts, including such unusual monsters as the giant rays.

For commercial use, Florida waters yield everything from menhaden, valuable for its oil and fertilizer, to pearls found in both freshwater and saltwater molluscs. Oysters even grow on trees in the mysterious Ten Thousand Islands near Naples.

Even the manatees have returned to Florida. In early days these strange "sea cows" could be seen in Manatee Springs feeding on the succulent water plants. They disappeared for many years, but recently have been seen at the spring again. The manatee may have created the legend of mermaids. Sailors seeing these unglamorous creatures at a great distance sunning on a rock excitedly thought they were seeing fishlike beauties from the deep.

OTHER TREASURES

The worth of Florida's rich soils, warm climate, and water resources cannot be measured by dollar value, but they continue to be the state's greatest natural assets. This is especially true since they are found in almost exactly the right combinations.

Florida is not generally noted for its minerals, although phosphate deposits are outstanding. Limestone and clays, titanium ores, zircon, monazite, garnet sands, rutile, and ilmenite all are found.

Although test drilling continues both on land and offshore, no worthwhile deposits of oil or natural gas have yet been found in Florida.

The People Use Their Treasures

Florida calls itself "America's last frontier." While this may be more romantic than factual, it is quite true that the state's recent development and potential for further development are extraordinary.

The intensive development has come only within the last generation. In the period between 1930 and 1950 Florida was the fastest growing state in the nation. It continues to be a leading state in the percentage of its population growth, and only California surpasses it in actual population increase. In 1940 Florida had the smallest population of the twelve southeastern states. By 1960 Florida had reversed the field and led those same states in total population.

In the period between 1950 and 1961 the personal income of Floridians rose 185.8 percent, the largest increase in the nation and twice the national rate.

GOLDEN CITRUS

To the tourist waking one morning in the heart of Florida's orange country nothing could be more refreshing than the delicate scent of the citrus blossoms. But to the people of the state this scent of

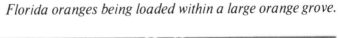

Florida oranges being loaded within a large orange grove.

blossoms means more than fragrance. Citrus brings more revenue to the state than any other single product.

Florida citrus production is one of the amazing agricultural achievements of the world, equaling the combined total production of California, Arizona, and Texas. Even more amazing, the tonnage of Florida's oranges, grapefruit, and tangerines is nearly a third larger than the combined tonnage of all the rest of the fruit produced in the entire United States. Florida citrus income averages considerably more than a billion dollars per year.

The early Spaniards brought oranges to Florida and planted them with the first settlement of St. Augustine in 1565. By the early 1800s growers had begun to ship the fruit commercially. By 1886 production for the first time had reached an annual total of a million boxes. Production had grown to five million boxes by 1894-95, when a freeze completely wrecked the industry. It took the industry almost fifteen years to regain its former strength.

The grapefruit has been a comparatively recent development. The first Florida grove was not planted until 1809, and the pink seedless grapefruit was not developed until 1913.

The greatest growth of the citrus industry has come in the last twenty years when methods of processing made possible easier shipment and storage. In 1950 the development of frozen concentrates by the Florida Citrus Commission and the later development of fresh juice in cartons and other improvements have caused mammoth growth. As a public service, the patent on citrus frozen concentrates was assigned by the Florida Citrus Commission to the people of the United States, through the Department of Agriculture.

The materials left over after processing are all used. Peels, pulp, and seeds are ground with minerals to produce a nourishing cattle

The citrus production from Florida's huge citrus groves (opposite) equals the combined total production of California, Arizona, and Texas.

feed. Citrus peel oils, seed oils, and even ethyl alcohol are produced from citrus leftovers.

Citrus growers have joined together in one of the most powerful associations of its kind, the Florida Citrus Mutual. This has been called the "best informed agricultural producer in the world," because of its research and informational programs. There are more than 12,000 grower-members.

The freezes of the winter of 1962-63 brought disaster to the Florida citrus industry, but a carefully planned program lessened the effects and brought a quick recovery.

LIKE JACK'S BEANSTALK

When the temperatures dropped unofficially to 8 degrees Fahrenheit (-13.3 degrees Celsius) in Florida in 1895 the citrus industry was temporarily ruined. H.M. Flagler immediately shipped carloads of all kinds of vegetable seeds to aid Florida agriculturalists. This was the beginning of large-scale vegetable growing in the state. Today the state is one of the vegetable markets of the world, with twenty varieties of vegetables in large-scale commercial growth. These include beans, cabbage, celery, cucumbers, eggplant, radishes, escarole, peppers, potatoes, squash, and others. Florida's climate permits more than one crop per year, so production is high per acre.

Tomatoes rank next after citrus as the most valuable single crop in Florida. After citrus, the largest acreage is planted in Florida's sweet red watermelons. Field crops such as corn, cotton, oats, hay, peanuts, soybeans, and tobacco add many millions of dollars to Florida's annual income.

Until the federal government placed an embargo on the import of Cuban sugar, about a third of this country's sugar came from Cuba. Now Florida's Sugar Cane Growers Cooperative is working hard to increase domestic production of sugarcane. Acreage has been increased, and huge harvesters lumber over the fields, lifting the cane stalks into enormous trailer trains that roll on twenty huge wheels.

Florida cowboys take a break from their daily routine to have fun at a rodeo.

The dairy industry is the third largest agricultural pursuit in the state.

Florida is already an important state in beef production, and this business is growing all the time. The business got its start during the Cuban revolt against Spain, beginning about 1868. Picturesque Florida cowboys received the name "Crackers" from the long whips that they cracked. The snorting Brahman cattle with their big humps have become a symbol of Florida livestock. The Brahman Breeders Association is located at Ocala.

Many thoroughbred horses are raised in Florida. The fine, white-fenced thoroughbred ranches also are centered in the Ocala region and have produced such famous racers as Kentucky Derby winners Needles and Carryback.

Another business in more unusual "livestock" is carried on in the Lake Okeechobee region where swamps are fenced and catfish are raised for sale along with huge bullfrogs, which are sent to market for those who prize frogs' legs as food.

Although agriculture looms large in Florida's economy, it has so many unrealized possibilities that it may be said agriculture is still only an infant there. Almost anything can happen in a land where such exotic crops as tung oil, papaya, mango, and sea grapes are commonplace.

GETTING MORE INDUSTRIOUS

Although Florida is not yet one of the leading states in manufacturing, in the five-year period from 1957 through 1961 almost four thousand new industries came to the state. In almost the same period the value of manufacturers increased 84.3 percent. The number of jobs for workers in industry actually doubled in the period between 1950 and 1960. At present, Florida manufacturers each year produce nearly fifteen billion dollars worth of products.

Manufacturers of food products are the largest manufacturing group, with electrical equipment second.

One of Florida's earliest and most colorful industries was that of cigar making. Cuban cigar makers, having difficulties in the insurrection against Spain, moved to Key West, and by 1870 that community was the largest cigar manufacturing center in the world. Strange as it may seem now, Key West then had the largest population in all of Florida. By 1886 cigar making had shifted to Tampa.

Because of Cape Canaveral, all businesses related to space and electronics have expanded rapidly in Florida. Many hundreds of Florida firms deal with testing, research, electronics, aircraft, missiles, scientific instruments, and nucleonics. In addition, hundreds of firms specialize in engineering.

Because of the tremendous growth and ideal conditions, experts now predict that within a few years Florida will become one of the country's major manufacturing states.

BARKING UP THE RIGHT TREES

Florida's live oaks were invaluable in the shipbuilding industry until wooden ships were no longer used.

It was necessary to bury live oak timbers in the mud for several years to season them. Sometimes these were forgotten or abandoned in the mud, and many an excavator has been surprised to uncover a neat pile of well-preserved timber.

During the 1880s Jacksonville became the world center for naval stores. Turpentine and resin are still valuable products of Florida forests. To collect turpentine a skilled axman strips off about a foot (.3 meter) of bark and sapwood from the pine, tapering toward the bottom. At the bottom of this cut a spout is driven in, with a cup to collect the sap. Several days pass before the cups are filled and then emptied into barrels which are taken to stills where the turpentine is distilled. The residue left after distillation is the resin.

Cutting of pulp and papermaking are today's leaders in the Florida wood products field.

One of Florida's fastest-growing trees is the gumbo-limbo of the Keys. Its sap is used to make such different kinds of products as medicine and mucilage.

Altogether, forest products bring to Florida each year the substantial sum of nearly a billion dollars.

NOT SUCH A LITTLE SHRIMP

Creatures of the sea provide a living for many Florida people. Commercial fishing has always been among Florida's most picturesque activities.

In the late 1940s large shrimp beds were discovered off the Dry Tortugas, and since then, the largest Florida shrimp catches have come from this area.

The sponge industry once was centered at Key West. The sponge fisherman would look at the bottom through a glass-bottomed bucket and then would hook the sponge with a long pole. This could be done only in relatively shallow water.

In 1905 a group of sponge fishermen from the Greek islands came to Florida and settled at Tarpon Springs. Ever since that time this has been one of the most interesting and picturesque communities of the

Sponge fishermen ply their trade at Tarpon Springs.

United States. For centuries the Greek divers had been trained to harvest sponges from even very deep water. New diving equipment has taken some of the risk from this occupation, and artificial sponges have captured much of the market, but the sponge fishermen continue to ply their trade at Tarpon Springs.

MINERALS

Florida has had only one mining "boom." In 1888 high-grade phosphate rock was discovered near Dunnellon. Prospectors quickly opened up the back country in search of this valuable fertilizer material.

Florida now leads the nation in the production of phosphate. In fact the state produces the tremendous total of 72 percent of all United States output. Florida is also first in the production of zirconium, staurolite, and fuller's earth.

Key Largo limestone is a beautiful building stone. Other limestones, sand, and gravel also are important. Florida sand can be separated from a number of minerals which make valuable by-products of the sand business.

TRANSPORTATION AND COMMUNICATION

One of the reasons Florida remained undeveloped for so long was the fact that transportation inland was almost impossible. The Old Spanish Trail had its western end in San Diego and its eastern terminus in St. Augustine, but Florida's section of it fell into disuse, and coastal and river boats carried most of the freight and traffic.

Then in the 1830s railroads began to take over the burden.

One of the world's milestones in transportation was the opening of the overseas railroad to Key West. The hurricane of 1935 caused so much damage to the right-of-way that the railroad was abandoned.

This railroad, with its stupendous bridges, was used as a base for another of the world's engineering triumphs — the highway that went to sea. The remarkable road was completed in 1938.

More than four hundred years after De Soto first entered the great bay of Tampa, modern-day explorers on the Sunshine Skyways drive across the very waters where his boats once sailed. This combination of bridge and causeway was finished in 1954.

In spite of the improvement in land transportation, ocean transport maintains its importance. No point in the state of Florida is more than 100 miles (161 kilometers) from an oceangoing port. Miami's Metropolitan Seaport in Biscayne Bay was opened in 1964.

The Jacksonville Shipyard attracts large ships from all over the world.

Miami International Airport

Even more dramatic has been the growth of transportation in the air. Miami's mammoth International Airport has been called "the greatest international air transport center in the world."

In the field of communication, the first Florida newspaper was the *East Florida Gazette,* of St. Augustine, founded in 1783. Florida daily papers today include the *Miami Herald* and *Miami Daily News,* the *Tribune* and *Times* of Tampa, and the *Journal* and *Times Union* of Jacksonville.

SUNSHINE FOR SALE

In spite of the great values of agriculture, manufacturing, and minerals, Florida's greatest income comes from a product that has never been grown, bottled, crated, juiced, mined, manufactured, or canned. It is the pure enchantment of sunshine of the sparkling seashores and gemlike islands, the wildlife vying with the night life, the magic of nature combined with the magic of Disney and other man-made attractions.

Each year more than thirty million tourists spend an incredible total of nearly ten billion dollars in Florida.

64

Human Treasures

REMARKABLE INDIANS

Few Americans have had a more unusual and interesting history than the famous Indian leader Osceola. Although not a chief, he was one of the leading Indian figures in American history.

Those who knew him gave him high tribute for ability and intelligence. During the Second Seminole War he had probably no more than a thousand followers and yet he and his men kept at bay ten thousand United States soldiers, led by seven ranking officers.

In October, 1837, Osceola asked for a conference with army leaders. He came forward under a flag of truce and was captured by the army. This government action was called "perfidious" by the *New York Herald*. The *Herald* said that if Osceola had not been captured contrary to the laws of war, the conference he called might have ended the Second Seminole War. Others have said that the Indians were in violation of their sacred treaties and deserved any treatment they got.

Later Osceola was sent to Fort Moultrie near Charleston, South Carolina. There he became ill. When he knew that he was dying, Osceola called for his full war costume, including his hunting knife. In full dress, surrounded by his wives and children, he made a statement of his attitude toward his friends and enemies and died at the age of thirty-four.

But even after his death his white brothers were not finished with his humiliation. The head of this Indian leader was severed from his body, embalmed, and given to the Surgical and Pathological Museum of Valentine Mott. There it was exhibited with a catalog listing "Miscellaneous—No. 1132. Head of Osceola, the great Seminole Chief (undoubted). Presented by Dr. Whitehurst of St. Augustine." When the museum burned in 1866, many of the collections were destroyed, apparently including this gruesome relic of a brave Seminole.

Osceola is honored by a display in the Castillo de San Marcos in St. Augustine. This includes a plaster cast of his face made after death.

His body was not returned to his home state for burial but remains at Fort Moultrie.

After Osceola's death, the Seminole War leadership turned to Chief Coacoochee. He had been captured with Osceola and imprisoned in Castillo de San Marcos, but had managed to escape. Coacoochee was much respected by his people. After having accepted Christianity he kept track of the Sabbath with a notched stick. He would not permit his followers to have any strong drink or entertainment on the holy day.

In one of his raids, Coacoochee captured a carriage and baggage wagon on the road to St. Augustine. Soon after that, Coacoochee was invited to a council. To the great astonishment of everyone who saw him, he appeared in the imposing, flowing robes of a

Statue of Indian leader Osceola at Silver Springs.

Shakespearean costume. He had captured the baggage of a traveling theatrical company. On several later occasions this Indian leader appeared in various theatrical costumes.

When Coacoochee was captured in 1841, the Second Seminole War was brought near its close.

Another well-publicized Indian of the Seminole Wars was a young Indian boy, Charlie, who tried to warn his friends of the Colee family that the Indians planned to massacre them. He failed, and the family was killed. To punish Charlie the tribal council banished him and had his ears cut off. He lived well into the twentieth century and became a familiar figure in Miami, Fort Lauderdale, and Palm Beach, where he was called "Crop-Eared Charlie."

One of Florida's most remarkable Indian leaders was Alexander McGillivray, son of a Seminole woman and a Scottish trader. He rose to the rank of colonel in the British army during the Revolution. He died in 1793 after holding "high commissions under three great civilized powers."

ICE AND MUDD

Two well-known men associated with Florida were physicians, but their careers could hardly have been more different.

Dr. John Gorrie practiced medicine in Apalachicola. During the hot days of summer, his patients in the hospitals suffered terribly.

Dr. Gorrie invented, and patented in 1855, the first machine for making artificial ice. Although his ice machine made Dr. Gorrie "one of the great benefactors of the human race," according to some authorities, he had received little recognition before his death in 1855. However, Dr. Gorrie was one of the two Florida men selected to represent the state in the hall of fame in Statuary Hall at the national Capitol building.

Dr. Samuel A. Mudd came to Florida as a federal prisoner. When John Wilkes Booth came to the doctor to have him set the leg he had broken when he killed President Abraham Lincoln, Dr. Mudd set it without knowing who Booth was or how he had broken his leg.

Mudd was sentenced unjustly to life imprisonment as one of the Lincoln conspirators and sent to Fort Jefferson in the Dry Tortugas.

Dr. Mudd worked so heroically to control a yellow fever epidemic on the island that he was pardoned in 1869.

GIANTS: EAST AND WEST

H. B. Plant had made a fortune in the transportation field. He developed railroads on the west coast of Florida, but he also did outstanding work in the hotel field there.

Harrison M. Flagler had made his fortune in oil in the North, but he had always wanted to build hotels and railroads. He came to Florida and built the Ponce de Leon Hotel at St. Augustine and then the Alcazar, finished in 1888. These were considered the finest resort hotels ever built until that time. Later, his developments in Palm Beach helped make it the "social capital of the world."

In order to bring customers to his hotels, Flagler found that the railroad system needed improvement. He gradually built and consolidated railroad lines until he reached Miami. When he decided to build a railroad to Key West, skeptics called it "Flagler's Folly." In spite of government interference, storms, and financial panic Flagler pushed his railroad out to sea.

In 1912, after seven years of building, the road was finished, and Flagler, at the age of eighty-two, triumphantly rode the first train into a celebrating Key West. He died the following year.

WORDS AND PICTURES

One of the earliest Europeans ever to live in Florida, the French artist Jacques Le Moyne, turned out and later published a remarkable number of drawings revealing the Florida scene.

An accomplished nature artist was an Englishman, Mark Catesby, who traveled in Florida from 1724 to 1728. One of the most extraordinary things about Catesby's work is that in his two-volume book he left fine drawings of most of the native Florida reptiles, fish, birds, plants, and animals known today. This is a scientific and artistic accomplishment few have equaled. His beautiful work may still be seen in some Florida libraries.

A father and son team of naturalists visited Florida in 1765 and 1766. John Bartram and his son William recorded characteristics of many ornamental and useful plants that had been unknown until that time. William Bartram traveled in Florida again in 1774 and added to the knowledge of the country.

The most famous artist-naturalist to visit Florida was John James Audubon. One authority has said of him, "No finer accounts have ever been written of primeval Florida than those from his gifted pen, and we are indebted to him for such information of general conditions in this country as could only come from a scholar and observer of great ability."

American writers early discovered the Florida climate. William Cullen Bryant and Ralph Waldo Emerson were among the first tourists ever to soak up the winter sunshine there.

John James Audubon, the well-known artist-naturalist, visited Florida and captured much of the state's wildlife in his paintings.

Ernest Hemingway maintained a home at Key West, where he did much of his writing.

Tennessee Williams and Ernest Hemingway maintained homes at Key West. Hemingway's novel *To Have and Have Not* has its setting in Key West. Many of his famous works were written there, including *Winner Take Nothing, Green Hills of Africa, The Fifth Column,* and *The Snows of Kilimanjaro.* He also started *For Whom the Bell Tolls* while living there.

Marjorie Kinnan Rawlings wrote of her Florida home in *Cross Creek* and in *The Yearling.*

INTERESTING PEOPLE

Florida's General Edmund Kirby Smith became one of the seven full generals of the Confederate army. He is the only other Florida man besides Dr. John Gorrie whose statue stands in Statuary Hall in the Capitol building in Washington. He was the last Confederate general to surrender—forty-five days after Lee surrendered at Appomattox.

General William Wing Loring of St. Augustine served in the Confederate army, but the most unusual part of his career was his service as grand commander of the army of Egypt.

Royalty came to Florida in 1824 when Napoleon Murat, prince of Naples and nephew of Napoleon Bonaparte, bought an estate near Tallahassee. He was twenty-three years old. He married a seventeen year old widow, grandniece of George Washington. They went to

70

Belgium for a visit, but the popular prince looked so much like his uncle that the Belgian government requested him to leave. After a social triumph in England, they returned to the United States in 1834. He wrote an interesting book about life in the United States at the time. When he died in 1847, his widow continued to live in Florida, but the Civil War wiped out her fortune. She lived in poverty until Napoleon III of France gave her a pension. She died in Tallahassee in 1867.

Among the early landholders of Florida, Dr. Andrew Turnbull was one of the best known. He received a grant of 60,000 acres (24,281 hectares) from the English king. He used his own fortune, the fortune of his lovely Greek wife, and investments from many wealthy Englishmen to establish the colony of New Smyrna.

As one commentator has said, "He colonized it with wild mountaineers from southern Greece, Italian convicts, and peasants of mixed Catalonian, Moorish, and Spanish blood from the Balearic Islands." The great plantations he established were to grow sugarcane and indigo for dyes. Though he constructed a brilliantly engineered drainage system, some of which still works today, and made many other improvements, the "wild" people who worked for him and the "wild" country proved too much, and the experiment failed.

Harry B. Lum tried to start a coconut plantation on the site of Miami Beach in 1882, but rabbits ate the young coconut shoots as soon as they came up, and the plan was unsuccessful.

William P. Duval, second governor of Florida Territory, was made famous by Washington Irving, whose character Ralph Ringwood portrayed Duval's early adventures. Another contemporary writer said Duval "was a man and no mistake. Nature made him with her sleeves rolled up. You couldn't sit ten minutes in his company without feeling that he was one of God Almighty's gentlemen, belonging to the aristocracy of Nature." Another said, "He was equally at home in the pioneers' cabin or in the most select circles of high society, brave as a lion and prepared for any emergency." Powerful Chief Neamathla said of Duval, "He never spake with a forked tongue."

Above: Florida Southern College, Lakeland.
Right: The spectacular Tampa Bay Hotel with
its Moorish towers now houses the University
of Tampa. Below: The oldest wooden
schoolhouse in the United States, St. Augustine.

Teaching and Learning

Florida became one of the first states to have a state educational organization when the Florida Education Society was established in 1831. The first state school system was organized in 1849.

The University of Florida, at Gainesville, was established in 1905. Included in the work of the university is the Florida Agricultural Experiment Station, a part of the School of Forestry. One of the most complete collections of plants is to be found in the Kirby-Smith Herbarium. The university also maintains the P.K. Yonge School, a model laboratory for teacher training from kindergarten through high school.

Other state institutions include Florida State University at Tallahassee; University of South Florida, Tampa; Florida Agricultural and Mechanical University, Tallahassee; and Florida Atlantic University, Boca Raton.

A unique Florida institution is the Florida Institute for Continuing Studies. This is an advanced graduate program set up with the cooperation of the various state four-year schools.

Included among Florida's many private four-year and graduate colleges are the University of Tampa; the University of Miami, Coral Gables; Stetson University, De Land; Rollins College, Winter Park; Bethune-Cookman College, Daytona Beach; and Jacksonville University, Jacksonville.

One of the most interesting college campuses in Florida is that of Florida Southern College at Lakeland. Its extraordinary chapel and other buildings were designed by the famed architect Frank Lloyd Wright.

Another of the unusual colleges in Florida is Bethune-Cookman. It was founded in 1904 by Mary McLeod Bethune, as she herself said, "with five girls, a small cabin, $1.50 and a million dollars' worth of faith. We used charred splinters as pencils. For ink we mashed up elderberries." Bethune merged with Cookman Institute in 1922.

Altogether there are twenty-seven accredited four-year colleges and universities in Florida.

The oldest house in historic St. Augustine.

Enchantment of Florida

Those who think of Florida only as a pleasant land of fine hotels, beaches, sun, and surf are surprised by the extraordinary variety of the state's further attractions.

ST. AUGUSTINE

The visitor who passes through the quaint and interesting gates of St. Augustine and drives slowly up the narrow street finds himself in a wholly different world. The memories of four hundred years of history alone are enough to fascinate even the most uninterested. In 1965 St. Augustine marked its 400th birthday with a year-long anniversary celebration. Some of the families still living there can trace their history in St. Augustine nearly as far back as the founding of the city in 1565.

Although they look more ancient, the city's gates were not built until 1804. Other gates had been constructed at an earlier time. In those days, the gates were closed at dusk. If a picnic party returned after dark, the women and children could go in, but the men had to stay outside all night.

Today the narrow streets are still lined with buildings. The oldest house in St. Augustine is a popular attraction, although this is not the oldest house ever built in the United States. None of the earliest houses in the oldest city have been preserved until our time, since the city was destroyed on several occasions.

Horse-drawn surreys carry visitors on tours of the city's attractions. For their Easter parade, the horses of St. Augustine are dressed up in their finest Easter bonnets.

Castillo de San Marcos is the oldest masonry fort still existing in the United States. The castle was begun by the Spanish in 1672 and was not finished until 1756. The material in its finishing coat is one of the finest ever used. Unfortunately, its formula has been lost.

For more than a hundred years after the United States took over in Florida, the castle was called Fort Marion, in honor of Francis

Marion, but the historic old name was restored. It became a National Monument in 1924.

In that same year, 350 years after his death, St. Augustine was given the grave marker and the casket from which the body of its founder, Pedro Menéndez de Avilés, had been taken in Puerto Rico. Now in the fall each year, St. Augustine recreates the coming of its founder and his conquistadores. Once again they sail into Matanzas Bay and claim the land for Spain, and a two-day observance follows.

In the heart of St. Augustine, Plaza de la Constitucion is known as the oldest public square in the United States. One of the Civil War cannon displayed in the park is said to be still loaded.

Probably the most complete restoration of an old-time general store is St. Augustine's "Oldest Store." In the storeroom of the C.F. Hamblen store was found a wonderful collection of venerable merchandise. The famous old store was turned into a museum of early-day merchandising, showing stocks of patent medicines, kerosene lamps, meat, whiskey, horse collars, churns, and wax cylinder records for old-time talking machines.

St. Augustine's restoration of an old-time general store is a museum and popular tourist attraction.

Other St. Augustine attractions are the Old Spanish Inn and the modern statue of Father Lopez, by famed sculptor Ivan Mestrovic. Father Lopez probably offered the first parish mass in what is now the United States. An extensive restoration of old buildings will continue until much of the old city has been restored.

The oldest and largest alligator farm in the country (6,000 alligators) is claimed for St. Augustine, and the ostrich farm there also draws many visitors.

Across the Matanzas River is Anastasia Island, where some of the natural setting of the region has been preserved in Anastasia State Park.

Somewhat farther south is Fort Matanzas National Monument, near the site where Ribaut's men were slaughtered by the Spanish.

ANDREW JACKSON'S VILLAGE

If the Ribaut settlement had not been destroyed, the Jacksonville area might have claimed the first permanent settlement in Florida. The modern city was named in honor of the American "patron saint" of Florida, Andrew Jackson. A fine memorial to Ribaut may be seen at Jacksonville. The famed writer Harriet Beecher Stowe maintained her winter home there for more than twenty years and helped to establish the Church of Our Savior there.

Modern Jacksonville is an energetic city with fine superhighways and a thriving business community. Its many cultural centers include the Cummer Gallery of Art and the Civic Auditorium.

Some nearby points of interest are Little Talbot Island State Park; Fort George, home of John McIntosh, president of the "Republic of East Florida" in 1812; and Fort Caroline Memorial. The original location of Fort Caroline was long ago washed into the sea; the memorial is located as near as possible to the original site.

Fort Clinch State Park forms the most northeasterly part of Florida. Named for General Duncan L. Clinch, it is a combined military-nature-seaside park. The fort was begun in 1850 and not finished by the time of the Civil War.

SUNSWEPT SEASHORE

From Fort Clinch to Key West, the visitor can drive all the way along one of the most varied and interesting coastlines in the world.

A major attraction is Marine Studios at Marineland. In this first display of its kind in the world, large sea creatures swim around in huge tanks almost as freely as they would in the ocean. It was here that the first studies of porpoises began to show how truly intelligent these creatures are. The porpoise demonstrations are still a highlight of a visit to Marineland. Florida has more such oceanariums than any other state. Others are Gulfarium at Fort Walton Beach, Theater-of-the-Sea in Islamorada, and Seaquarium in Miami.

Continuing down the sunswept seashore, the visitor will find Bulow Plantations Historical Memorial at Flagler Beach.

Near Ormond Beach is Tomoka State Park, with its strange and unique statue that tells the legend of the Indian Chief Tomokie.

Daytona Beach claims to have the most famous beach in the world. Here, for mile after mile, cars may be driven along the water's edge on hard, smooth sands.

Many world speed records have been set here, including the world auto mark of almost 70 miles (113 kilometers) per hour achieved by Alexander Winton in his "Bullet" in 1903, when most people had never yet seen an automobile. Daytona Beach's racing history is remembered in the Museum of Speed, where one of the prized exhibits is the famous "Bluebird" auto in which Sir Malcolm Campbell set what was then the land speed record of 276 miles (444 kilometers) per hour in 1935. Today auto racing is carried on at the Daytona Speedway, one of the world's most noted tracks.

In 1873 a ship carrying a cargo of coconuts and wine was wrecked on a long narrow island on the southern Florida coast. The wreck came about because the crew had gotten into the wine cargo, drinking so much they lost control of the ship. Later the shipwrecked coconuts sprouted, and the beautiful palm trees that grew up from them gave the area its name of Palm Beach. Now the city's famous palms produce so many coconuts that West Palm Beach spends ten thousand dollars each year just to dispose of them. In 1893 H.M.

78

Miles and miles of hotels and motels with beachfront cabanas in Miami Beach attract visitors from all over the world.

Flagler built his great Royal Poinciana Hotel there. Today the area is one of secluded and fabulous estates. Whitehall, Mr. Flagler's own mansion at West Palm Beach, has been made a museum.

Royal Poinciana Boulevard, which is lined with magnificent poinciana trees, is an unforgettable Palm Beach sight when the trees are covered with scarlet blooms.

Fort Lauderdale is called the "Venice of America." There are 270 miles (434 kilometers) of waterways within the city limits. Its Promenade de Paris is one of the liveliest annual carnivals in Florida.

In Fort Lauderdale is Hugh Taylor Birch State Park, and nearby is Okalee Seminole Indian Village.

Port Everglades has a deep harbor and is the principal port of southeast Florida.

CASTLES FOR THE TOURING KINGS

The visitor who drives down Collins Avenue in Miami Beach will see a unique collection of buildings—mile after mile of the most costly structures, vast hotels and motels, all with their cabana colony beach fronts. From the most garish to the most elegant, they are all designed to attract attention and to offer the visitor the last word in comfort, relaxation, and entertainment.

Miami itself is also a city of fine homes, great hotels, and fine stores. It was first visited by Menéndez in 1567; he found a large Indian village there.

The area remained very much in its original state until almost the twentieth century. In the 1890s an Ohio woman, Mrs. Julia D. Tuttle, became very fond of the Miami region. She wrote, "It may seem strange, but it is the dream of my life to see this wilderness turned into prosperous country and where this tangled mass of vines, brush, trees and rocks now are, to see homes, surrounded by beautiful grassy lawns."

She helped to persuade H.M. Flagler to build his railroad to her "wilderness," and when Mr. Flagler became interested in the area, the region began the growth that has continued ever since.

The Dade County Art Museum in Miami is housed in Vizcaya, one of the most spectacular mansions in America. Vizcaya is the former home of James Deering. Another unique attraction is the Japanese garden in Watson Park, donated to the city by the Japanese industrialist, Kiyoshi Ichimura.

Fairchild Tropical Gardens, with the largest collection of tropical plants in the United States, are noted for their stand of Royal Palms, grown from seed to maturity in only twenty years.

An interesting commercial attraction is the Monkey Jungle. Here the monkeys run free through the jungle growth, and the visitors are "caged." That is, the paths are all covered with heavy wire mesh so that the monkeys cannot get to the visitors, or the other way around.

At the parrot jungle may be seen one of the world's largest collections of tropical birds, including more than a hundred flamingos. Flamingos are also one of the many attractions of Hialeah Park racetrack near Miami. Other Miami area attractions are the Seaquarium, Wax Museum, and Serpentarium.

KEYS TO ENCHANTMENT

The visitor who heads south from Miami on the Overseas Highway across the Florida Keys will have one of the world's most

Beautiful tropical sunsets like this one are commonplace along the Florida seacoast.

interesting experiences. The word Key comes from "cay," meaning little island. Though there are about a thousand of these little islands, only sixty-two are populated. For a time the Keys had a larger population than the Florida mainland.

The first and largest island on the highway is Key Largo. This key is headquarters for America's most unusual national park—Key Largo Coral Reef Preserve. The state's portion is called John Pennekamp Coral State Park. This park is almost entirely under the ocean, and is the first underseas park within the continental United States.

President Dwight Eisenhower proclaimed the area a national park in 1960. Here are about 75 miles (121 kilometers) of living coral formations. The park was formed to protect the coral from coral hunters who were rapidly ripping it all from the sea for souvenirs. About 30 different species of coral are found there. Beneath the clear waters may be seen the beautiful statue of Christ of the Abysses, donated by the Underwater Society of America. This is a duplicate of a statue found beneath the waters of the harbor of Genoa, Italy.

The name "Key West" does not come from a Spanish phrase meaning "Western Island." Instead it comes from the Spanish words *cayo hueso,* meaning "Isle of Bones." The many bones found there were thought to be those of Indians killed in battle.

In the 1830s Key West was said to be the richest city in the country per capita. The numerous shipwrecks of the area contributed to this wealth. Men, called "the wreckers," made fortunes from the misfortunes of others. Most of the wreckers were considered an evil lot, and were said to have misled ships on their routes in order to wreck them and get the cargoes. The famous naturalist, John J. Audubon, spent much time in the area, and he disputes this reputation of the wreckers. He found that they often helped to save vessels.

America's first international commercial aviation began at Key West with Pan American's route to Havana, Cuba.

Visitors see the sights of Key West on the famous Conch Train tours. Among the interesting attractions are the Naval Base, founded in 1822; President Truman's Little White House; and the fascinating turtle crawls, where great turtles are kept on their way to becoming soup and turtle steak. Other eating delights of the Keys are its noted key melons and key limes.

Sixty miles (ninety-six kilometers) west of Key West are the seldom visited Dry Tortugas, home of Fort Jefferson National Park,

The ruins of Fort Jefferson on Garden Key in the Dry Tortugas.

where the vast ruins of this great fort have been preserved. It was begun with the hope that it would become the "Gibraltar of the Caribbean." It was not finished because during its long period of construction warfare changed so much that it would have been almost useless.

MYSTERIOUS EVERGLADES

Florida's southern tip is a mysterious area of swampland and grassland, where birds, animals, and reptiles teem. In 1947 the federal government set this wonderful area apart for all time as a national park, the only one of its kind. Today, visitors can drive through the Everglades all the way to the southernmost city of the continental United States, Flamingo.

At various places wooden walkways have been built far into the swampy depths. Here the wildlife may be observed. Multitudes of water birds fly, fish, and sun themselves. Huge lords of the swamp, the alligators, may be seen resting on banks or moving along the surface of the water with only their knobby eyes and nostrils showing. Green lizards in the Everglades are often friendly and curious, and may approach a visitor.

For those who want an even closer inspection of the glades, the Audubon Society operates tours by boat and swamp buggy through some of the wildest areas of the country.

Descendants of the Seminole Indians who fled to the Everglades as a last refuge in the Second Seminole War still live here. Floridians like to say that the Seminole War is still going on because there never was a treaty of peace, although a truce was signed at the late date of 1938. In a sense the Seminole War is still going on, technically, but the modern-day Indians who live in Florida today are far from warlike.

Other points of interest in the Everglades area are the Everglades Wonder Gardens at Bonita Springs near Naples, and Collier-Seminole State Park near the Everglades. One of the most exciting events in the area is the annual Swamp Buggy Derby at Naples. Tall marsh buggies, on their huge airplane tires, splash through gooey mud in a contest of endurance for both driver and machine. Fleischmann Gardens has the world's only performing-water-bird show.

Descendants of the Seminole Indians who fled to the Everglades during the Second Seminole War still live here. This Indian village is along the Tamiami Trail in the Florida Everglades.

Beautiful Cypress Gardens, near Winter Haven, offers water shows daily.

HIGHWAY OF ORANGE BLOSSOMS

One of central Florida's main arteries is U.S. Highway 27. Because of the hundreds of orange groves nearby, it has been called the "Orange-Blossom Highway." For mile after mile the sweet scent of the blossoms follows the visitor.

Many state parks dot the central Florida area, including Highlands Hammock State Park, Sebring; Hillsborough River State Park, Zephyrhills; and Manatee Springs State Park, Chiefland.

Many of the central Florida cities are extremely attractive, but do not get the large crowds of visitors that go to both coasts. Orlando is the chief inland city of the region. It has the unusual distinction of having thirty lakes entirely within its city limits.

Kissimmee has one of the largest livestock markets in Florida and offers something of an "Old West" atmosphere because of its cattle country. Its bar was noted for its "saddle service," because ranch hands rode right up to it on their horses to be served. The flavor of the Old West is still retained in the Silver Spurs Rodeo at Kissimmee and the All Florida Rodeo at Arcadia.

World-famous Cypress Gardens offers not only a floral wonderland but also a water show that has been called the finest in the world, where some of the greatest water ski experts show their skill.

85

Lake Wales is the winter headquarters of the famous Black Hills Passion Play.

Farther north in the central area, Ocala National Forest protects the woodland resources of the state. At the southeast corner of the national forest is the scenic Alexander Springs.

Florida's most famous spring is Silver Springs, near Ocala. This is probably the most often-visited natural wonder of the state and also Florida's largest spring. Five hundred million gallons (nearly two billion liters) of crystal clear water pour from Silver Springs every day. Millions of visitors have enjoyed the glass-bottomed boat trips, watching the antics of the many fish and marveling at the many water plants, including a beautiful underwater evergreen tree and several flowering plants waving their fronds on the bottom.

On the banks of the Suwannee River at White Springs a memorial has been erected to Stephen Foster, the songwriter who made the river famous. His song "Old Folks at Home" contains the famous line, "Way down upon the Swanee river." That song is said to have made the Suwannee "the most romantic river in America."

In the Foster Memorial, dioramas illustrate the composer's most famous songs, and a magnificent carillon gives four daily concerts featuring his music. Every year there is a contest to select the most beautiful girl as "Miss Jeanie with the Light Brown Hair." Visitors may take a cruise on the romantic Suwannee in a miniature stern-wheeler, much like those of Foster's time. There is also a Suwannee River State Park.

The springs at White Springs were sacred to the Indians. Wounded warriors could treat their wounds in the waters of the springs without fear of attack.

FLORIDA'S WEST COAST

The west coast of Florida from the Keys to Pensacola was, at one time, a favorite haunt of pirates. Jean LaFitte and his associate Tavernier made their headquarters at the spot that is now the town of Tavernier.

One of the most famous pirates of all, Jose Gaspar, had his headquarters at Port Charlotte. An island in the harbor takes the name he gave himself—"Gasparilla." He is said to have killed all the men he captured and kept all the women. Captiva Island has been given its name because of the women captives held there.

Gasparilla has been called the "King of Pirates." He is said to have stolen as much as thirty million dollars in booty. Then in 1822 Gasparilla attacked a United States gunboat disguised as a merchant ship. He was defeated. Before he could be captured, Gasparilla wrapped himself in a heavy anchor chain and threw himself overboard.

One of the most remarkable of the pirates was William Augustus Bowles. During his lifetime he was a soldier, sailor, actor, portrait painter, and Indian chief as well as a pirate. He was highly thought of by the Indians and was given many honors by the British. He might have retired in England, wealthy and respected, but he returned to Florida and set up headquarters on St. George Island near Apalachicola. With a force of Indians and Europeans he attacked Fort St. Marks south of Tallahasee and captured this strongpoint after a six-week siege. By this time Bowles was so strong he was called the "King of Florida."

However, both Spain and the United States set out to conquer him and finally Bowles was delivered over to his Spanish enemies and sent as prisoner to Morro Castle in Havana. There he refused to eat and starved himself to death.

Captiva Island and its neighbor, Sanibel, now are quiet, popular resorts. The opening of a bridge to Sanibel in 1963 made this island more accessible. It is famed as one of the world's finest sources of seashells. More than three hundred varieties are found there, some of them extremely rare. Almost every visitor goes shelling on Sanibel and Captiva. Every wave coming to shore deposits another foot or so of shells along the southern and western beaches of the islands.

Thomas A. Edison spent almost fifty winters in Fort Myers. During the early days of electric lighting Edison offered to install street lights in Fort Myers. The city fathers refused because they said the light would keep the cows awake. Edison's home is maintained as a

FLORIDA

ATTRACTIONS IN FLORIDA'S 12 VACATION REGIONS

memorial, and visitors flock there to see the wonderful collection of rare and interesting tropical plants and flowers he assembled from all over the world, including the golden chalice vine.

Sarasota has retained many memories of the circus for which it was the winter headquarters. The circus family has contributed the great John and Mable Ringling Museum of Art. In connection with the museum is the Asolo Theater, the only eighteenth-century Italian theater in the United States, where operas and plays are performed. Sarasota is also the home of the Ringling Museum of the Circus.

88

Sarasota's Jungle Gardens are among the finest and best-known tropical gardens in Florida.

At nearby Bradenton, the DeSoto National Memorial was established in 1949. Near Bradenton is Skyway Memorial Gardens, where a reproduction of Leonardo da Vinci's Last Supper with life-sized figures has been carved in Carrara marble.

At Osprey, Mrs. Potter Palmer's famous palace-home, called The Oaks, is open to the public. Another home now on public view is the Gamble Mansion at Ellenton. This is where Confederate official Judah P. Benjamin took refuge at the end of the Civil War.

At Myakka River State Park, visitors see some of the 28,875 acres (11,685 hectares) by means of its famous ox-wagon tours. At the park is one of the largest bird rookeries known to exist. Remarkably, this rookery was not discovered until 1962.

One of the most colorful festivals of Florida is the annual "capture" of the Tampa area by the pirate Gasparilla. Everybody dresses in pirate costume. The full-rigged ship, *Jose Gasparilla,* sails into the bay. A wicked-looking crew of businessmen from the area, plus a few girl pirates, brandish cutlasses and shout. A downtown Tampa parade of pirates attracts close to a million spectators. The festival continues for a week, a feature of the great Florida State Fair in February.

Tampa now claims to have the finest harbor between Norfolk, Virginia, and New Orleans, Louisiana.

Busch Gardens at Tampa, founded by the brewing family, is said to have more visitors than any other attraction in Florida. The Moorish towers of the great Tampa Bay Hotel still startle visitors to downtown Tampa; the building is now the home of the University of Tampa.

To the north are two famous springs. Weekiwachee is noted for its stage show, where the theater is beneath the clear water. Homossassa Springs is called Nature's Giant Fish Bowl, because for some reason huge schools of ocean fish come seven miles (eleven kilometers) up the river to visit this spring. The various species do not mingle but come one at a time; when one variety leaves another arrives. Visitors may also watch this spectacle from under the water.

Cedar Key is one of Florida's most charming and lesser-known communities. Its long Florida history is recalled in its fine St. Clair Whitman Museum, which includes one of the most complete collections of shells ever assembled. At Port St. Joe the museum of the State Constitution Historic Memorial has many interesting exhibits.

PANHANDLE

The beauty of northwest Florida has been preserved in a large number of state parks. At O'Leno State Park, the Santa Fe River disappears beneath the ground, to reappear several miles away. There is also a natural bridge here. Other parks include Torreya State Park, Greensboro; St. Andrews State Park, Panama City; Falling Waters State Park; Fort Gadsden State Park, Sumatra; and Florida Caverns State Park, Marianna.

Tallahasee has been the capital of Florida since territorial days in 1823. The snowy white capitol building was begun in 1839. The old portion was finished in 1845. In 1901 the dome and two wings were added. Other additions came in 1923, 1937, and 1948. Tallahassee's oldest public building is the Presbyterian Church, completed in 1838.

At Apalachicola, the Gorrie Museum pays tribute to the modest Florida physician who invented ice making. There is a gleaming stretch of beach between Apalachicola and Pensacola.

At Pensacola, there is a reconstructed Spanish village of the period 1723-1754. This ancient town was old even before that time, and has some of the most interesting historical memories of the state. As almost everyone knows, the first United States naval air station was established at Pensacola. Almost everyone is surprised, however, to learn that this took place at the early date of 1914.

Nearby Fort Pickens State Park on Santa Rosa Island preserves the remains of that historic old fort.

Here, as elsewhere throughout the state, the visitor will find the enduring remains of history in our oldest continuously inhabited state, as well as the most up-to-date evidences of the space age.

Handy Reference Section

Instant Facts

Became the 27th state, March 3, 1845
Capital—Tallahassee
Nickname—The Sunshine State
Motto—"In God We Trust"
State flower—Orange Blossom
State bird—Mockingbird
State tree—Sabal Palmetto Palm
State song—"Old Folks at Home," sometimes called "Swanee River"
Area—58,560 square miles (151,670 square kilometers)
Rank in area—22nd
Greatest length (north to south)—507 miles (816 kilometers), Jacksonville to
                                 Key West; 832 miles (1,339 kilometers),
                                 Pensacola to Key West
Greatest width (east to west)—385 miles (620 kilometers)
Coastline—399 miles (642 kilometers), Atlantic; 798 miles (1,284 kilometers),
          Gulf Coast
Number of counties—67
Highest point—345 feet (105 meters)
Lowest point—Sea level
Population—11,156,820 (1978 est.)
Principal cities— Jacksonville   528,865 (1970 census)
                  Miami   334,859
                  Tampa   277,767
                  St. Petersburg   216,232
                  Fort Lauderdale 139,590
                  Hialeah   102,452
Population rank—9th
Population density—190.5 per square mile (73.5 per square kilometer), 1978 est.
Rank in density—14th

You Have a Date with History

1513—Ponce de León, first recorded European in Florida
1528—Narváez lands at Bahia Beach
1559—Tristán de Luna establishes colony on shores of Pensacola Bay
1564—René Laudonnière builds Fort Caroline
1565—St. Augustine founded by Menéndez; Protestants massacred
1586—Sir Francis Drake plunders and destroys St. Augustine
1600—Beginning of mission period
1698—Pensacola founded
1740—Oglethorpe invades Florida

1763—Florida becomes British in ransom for Havana
1783—Florida returned to Spanish in exchange for Bahamas
1814—Andrew Jackson captures Pensacola
1818—Jackson campaigns in Florida against outlaws
1821—Florida becomes American, with Jackson as governor
1824—Tallahassee chosen as capital
1835—Seminole War
1845—Statehood
1861—Florida withdraws from Union
1868—Florida restored to civil government
1884—Henry B. Plant brings consolidated railroad to Tampa
1896—Flagler railroad built to Miami
1898—Spanish American War brings renewed interest in Florida
1901—Jacksonville suffers great fire
1912—Railroad reaches Key West
1917—World War I training activities
1924—Land boom reaches its peak
1928—Tamiami Trail completed
1935—Two-hundred-mile-per-hour winds damage Keys
1941—Florida a World War II training and transportation center
1947—Minimum Foundation Program improves educational opportunities
1950—Frozen citrus crop; first missile launched in Florida
1962—John Glenn soars from Canaveral, first American in orbit
1963—Historic Cape Canaveral becomes Cape Kennedy
1965—St. Augustine celebrates 400th anniversary
1969—New state constitution is adopted
1969—Apollo II, the first spacecraft to land men on the moon, is launched from Cape Kennedy
1970—Environmental agency set up to review all proposed state projects
1973—Cape Kennedy renamed Cape Canaveral
1975—First two-nation space flight
1977—Tallahassee opens new state capitol

Governors of Florida

William D. Moseley 1845-1849
Thomas Brown 1849-1853
James E. Broome 1853-1857
Madison S. Perry 1857-1861
John Milton 1861-1865
A.K. Allison 1865
William Marvin 1865
David S. Walker 1865-1868
Harrison Reed 1868-1872
Ossian B. Hart 1873-1874
M.L. Stearns 1874-1877

George F. Drew 1877-1881
William D. Bloxham 1881-1885
Edward A. Perry 1885-1889
Francis P. Fleming 1889-1893
Henry L. Mitchell 1893-1897
William D. Bloxham 1897-1901
William S. Jennings 1901-1905
Napoleon B. Broward 1905-1909
Albert W. Gilchrist 1909-1913
Park Trammell 1913-1917
Sidney J. Catts 1917-1921

Cary A. Hardee 1921-1925
John W. Martin 1925-1929
Doyle E. Carlton 1929-1933
David Sholtz 1933-1937
Fred P. Cone 1937-1941
Spessard L. Holland 1941-1945
Millard F. Caldwell 1945-1949
Fuller Warren 1949-1953

Dan T. McCarty 1953
Charley E. Johns 1953-1954
LeRoy Collins 1954-1961
Farris Bryant 1961-1965
Haydon Burns, 1965-1967
Claude R. Kirk, Jr. 1967-1971
Reubin Askew 1971-1979
D. Robert Graham 1979-

Index

PICTURE CREDITS

Color photographs courtesy of the following: State of Florida, Department of Commerce, Division of Tourism, pages 8, 13, 14, 19, 21, 23, 33, 37, 43, 46, 57, 59, 62, 72, 74, and 88; USDI National Park Service, Castillo de San Marcos National Monument, 26; Library of Congress, 28; Walt Disney Productions, 45; USDI, Fish and Wildlife Service, 51; U.S. Department of the Army, Jacksonville District, Corps of Engineers, 63; USDI, National Park Service, Fort Jefferson National Monument, 83.

Illustrations on pages 69, 70, and back cover by Len W. Meents.

ABOUT THE AUTHOR

With the publication of his first book for school use when he was twenty, **Allan Carpenter** began a career as an author that has spanned more than 135 books. After teaching in the public schools of Des Moines, Mr. Carpenter began his career as an educational publisher at the age of twenty-one when he founded the magazine *Teachers Digest.* In the field of educational periodicals, he was responsible for many innovations. During his many years in publishing, he has perfected a highly organized approach to handling large volumes of factual material: after extensive traveling and having collected all possible materials, he systematically reviews and organizes everything. From his apartment high in Chicago's John Hancock Building, Allan recalls, "My collection and assimilation of materials on the states and countries began before the publication of my first book." Allan is the founder of Carpenter Publishing House and of Infordata International, Inc., publishers of *Issues in Education* and *Index to U. S. Government Periodicals.* When he is not writing or traveling, his principal avocation is music. He has been the principal bassist of many symphonies, and he managed the country's leading non-professional symphony for twenty-five years.